The Emergence of the Christian Basilica in the Fourth Century

The Emergence of the Christian Basilica in the Fourth Century

James Riley Strange

International Studies in Formative Christianity and Judaism
Global Publications, Binghamton University
2000

Library of Congress in Publication Data

James Riley Strange, *The Emergence of the Christian Basilica in the Fourth Century.*

ISBN 1-586840-32-0

Published and Distributed by:
International Studies in Formative Christianity and Judaism
Global Publications, Binghamton University
State University of New York at Binghamton
Binghamton, New York, USA 13902-6000
Phone: (607) 777-4495 or 777-6104; Fax: (607) 777-6132
E-mail: pmorewed@binghamton.edu
http://ssips.binghamton.edu

To my parents,
Jim and Carolyn Strange

James Riley Strange received his B.A. in Classics from Furman University, his M.Div. from Southern Baptist Theological Seminary, and his M.A. in Religious Studies from the University of South Florida. He is currently working on his Ph.D. in New Testament at Emory University.

Table of Contents

Acknowledgements

This monograph began as a research project in the Department of Religious Studies at the University of South Florida. I am greatly indebted to this department's faculty, and I wish to acknowledge it here. USF's Department of Religious Studies affords an ideal environment for learning. Its professors apparently have no trouble balancing both scholarly productivity and teaching excellence, and they freely give their attention to individual students.

I am especially grateful to two professors for the completion of this work: Jacob Neusner and James F. Strange. Dr. Neusner was my faculty advisor, the chair of my thesis committee, and more importantly, a continual source of wisdom, guidance, encouragement, and scholarly training. Under his direction Chapter 1 transformed from a jumble of information and false starts into a clear and coherent introduction of the problem at hand. Mostly, I owe him the debt of his unbending standards for excellence. Finally, I thank him, as Editor of the International Studies in Formative Christianity and Judaism series, for accepting this manuscript, and other articles of mine, for publication.

Dr. James F. Strange, my father, trained me in the specific skills necessary to complete the work, namely the use of archaeology and texts to explore social and religious problems. He closely read many drafts, and made several observations as to what, exactly, I needed to do in order to make my argument stick. Perhaps his greatest lesson to me has been to let the data speak for itself, not to argue for conclusions that the evidence does not support. That lesson seems fundamental now, but many times it has kept me from faulty methodology and shaky arguments.

To these two mentors I owe the highest debt of gratitude. I also wish to thank other USF faculty members with whom I studied and worked—Sara Mandell, Tamara Sonn, Danny Jorgensen, Paul Schneider, and Dell deChant—for providing an intellectually rigorous environment in which to labor.

I thank Margo Smith, my colleague and fellow Graduate Teaching Assistant in the department, for proofreading the manuscript for this monograph. She caught numerous errors and made many excellent suggestions of style and clarity. Her method was thorough and meticulous, as I knew it would be, and any errors that remain are my own.

Finally, I wish to thank Jim and Carolyn Strange, my parents, Mary Elizabeth Strange, Katherine Strange, and Joanna Strange, my sisters, and Laura and Sarah Smythe, who all have encouraged me and supported me in uncountable ways.

James Riley Strange
6 January, 2000
Tampa, Florida

List of Tables

List of Figures

Preface

I first hit upon the argument of this book when I was working on a separate problem. I was trying to determine if the Christian basilicas built in the fourth through seventh centuries in Palestine followed any particular plan. What I wanted to know was, did the dimensions of these basilicas show a constant ratio, and if they did, could I show that this plan followed the dictates of an ancient architect, such as Vitruvius. In 1970 Asher Ovadiah had published an exhaustive catalogue of churches built in the Holy Land between the fourth and seventh centuries, with later additions and updates in *Levant*, and I used his data to do my work.

I did discover some general patterns in the data. The most striking was that as the length of the building increases, the width of the nave itself remains relatively constant. This could be explained in more than one way, the simplest being that the width of the nave is controlled by the span of timbers available in the region and the cost of splicing a joist, since the splice requires additional supports and exponentially increases the amount of wood required. A second explanation is that the width of the nave reflects a certain ethos, that is, those who built basilicas thought that there was a "proper" width for a nave, for whatever reason.

While working out this problem, I made a more striking discovery that might help explain that ethos. The one defining characteristic that distinguished church basilicas from civil basilicas was the uniform orientation of the former on the long axis, and the arrangement of the interior space to control traffic. Certainly some civil basilicas were built this way, but many others surrounded the nave completely with colonnades. By contrast, nearly all Christian basilicas followed this plan. Removing the short aisles at either end and placing the main entrance in the short wall opposite the apse meant that upon entering the Christian basilica, one's eye was drawn down the length of the nave to the altar directly opposite the observer. Not only so, but it struck me that the altar was not simply the focus of attention, but the target of movement as well: if modern practices were at all applicable to late antiquity, the clergy entered the rear of the hall and approached the altar, then exited in the opposite direction. The very architecture invited pomp, movement in two directions, in and out.

Such a patter invited speculation, and I noticed that whereas the civil basilica resembled a roofed forum with four aisles completely surrounding the nave, the Christian basilica looked like a roofed section of a colonnaded street, such as the *cardo maximus*. I began to think of the Christian basilica as a "holy street," and I speculated on Mircea Eliade's ideas of the order and symmetry of sacred space versus the chaotic jumble of the profane.

I imagined a pilgrim who began outside a city such as Rome or Jerusalem in nature's organic muddle, and who encountered more and more signs of order, and thus of the Sacred, the closer he or she drew to the basilica. The first signs of order would be plowed fields with low stone walls and watchtowers, perhaps scattered farm buildings and houses. No doubt some homes spilled outside the city walls; the suburbs or villages near the city probably would not be constructed on a grid pattern, but the right angles of the buildings and the straight lines of the walls would interrupt nature. The first arresting sign of order would be the city wall, and once inside, symmetry and regularity would define the landscape. The straight lanes would form a grid, and the colonnaded sidewalks of the street would provide bilateral symmetry to the eye. The basilica church, then, seemed to be an extension of the street, but with even more imposed order to the exclusion of nature. The roof and walls would keep out weather and most of the noise and ambient light, making the basilica an enclosed environment by ancient standards, while the high roof over the nave mimicked an open structure. It was then that I remembered that the apses of many Byzantine and Medieval churches depict Christ enthroned in heaven, and the dome over the transept or ceiling over the nave sometimes show *putti* among the clouds with the resurrected Christ. I thought of Michelangelo's Sistine Chapel, and I noted the stars on the ceiling of a cathedral in Louisville, Kentucky.

All of this is supposition. In order to make the argument stick, to show that the design of the Christian basilica as a "holy street" is a reasonable hypothesis, I must demonstrate that people actually moved up and down the nave, toward the altar and away from it, in the way that the architecture suggests that they were meant to.

In the argument of this book I have eschewed the speculative language of "holy" or "sacred street," and have stuck rather to the data and the inferences that can be drawn from them. Namely, Christian basilicas from the very beginning follow a standardized design rather than many different designs, and I propose to answer why this is so. If we suppose that this standardization is deliberate, we ought to be able to infer what the design accomplishes, and we should be able to find evidence for it in the liturgy of the fourth century. Finally, we ought not to find the same standardized design in other types of basilicas, even religious basilicas, that did not house similar ritual activities.

Although I do not use this language in the book, the argument speculates on the idea of architecture as metaphor, or symbolic discourse. I begin with the assumption that no architecture not even domestic, agricultural, or industrial, is purely functional. Buildings mean something to those who build them, and to those who use them. That meaning is expressed in external form ("silhouette") and internal layout ("plan"). This book deals with the latter, and as I state in my conclusions, it deals with only one of the many possible metaphors at play in the design of the Christian basilica. I leave further exploration to other studies, whether they be mine or another's.

I turn now to the argument itself, beginning with a statement of the problem as I perceive it to be.

Chapter 1. Introduction to the Problem of the Christian Basilica

The Problem of Origins

In its major cities across the Empire, beginning some time in the second century B.C.E.,[1] and up to the fourth century C.E., Rome constructed public buildings called "basilicas." These were civil or municipal structures, housing the tribunal court and accommodating both private and public business in their broad, open halls. They were also associated with the *genus* of the Emperor: many displayed his effigy,[2] and Suetonius reports that as Augustus' body was transported back to Rome, it lay in state in temples and basilicas along the way.[3] In the fourth century C.E., Christians also began to construct basilicas for their purposes, and very soon nearly all monumental church buildings in the Empire took that form.[4] Thus the appearance of the

---

1 J.B. Ward-Perkins, "Constantine and the Origins of the Christian Basilica," *Papers of the British School at Rome*, 22 (1954): 71.

2 Richard Krautheimer, "The Beginning of Early Christian Architecture," in Krautheimer, *Studies in Early Christian, Medieval, and Renaissance Art* (New York: New York University Press; London: University of London Press, Ltd., 1969), 12; this article first appeared in *Review of Religion*, III (1939): 127-48; see also Krautheimer, "The Constantinian Basilica," *Dumbarton Oaks Papers*, No. 21 (Washington, DC: Dumbarton Oaks Center for Byzantine Studies, 1967), 123-4.

3 *VC* II,100.

4 For example, in his comprehensive work on Christian architecture in the first centuries C.E., Michael White treats all pre-fourth century church buildings—12 in all—that have been excavated or surveyed at various sites in the old Roman Empire (Europe, Greece, Asia Minor, Syria, Palestine, and North Africa). White demonstrates that none

Christian basilica in the fourth century presents a puzzle: for 500 years the Romans had been building basilicas; for the first three centuries of the common era Christians met in homes or small halls, but built no basilicas. During and after the fourth century, construction of civil basilicas appears virtually to have halted,[5] while Christians began to build nearly all their monumental churches in that form. Thus the first public Christian buildings appeared suddenly and spread quickly, and Christianity rapidly took over the basilical architectural style.

The Christian basilica presents four problems. First, we have to explain how a secular building became a religious building. Before the fourth century, the civil basilica served no overtly religious purpose; its lofty halls and interior

---

of these churches are basilicas; rather, all of them are some form of house church or small hall. Beginning in the late fourth century, however, basilicas were built over seven of these buildings, and I estimate that by the end of the fifth century there were over 100 basilicas across the Empire. Michael White, *The Social Origins of Christian Architecture*, Vol. II (Valley Forge: Trinity Press, Int'l., 1997); Richard Krautheimer *et al.*, *Corpus Basilicarum Christianarum Romae: The Early Christian Basilicas of Rome (IV-IX Cent.)*, Vols. I-V (Rome: Pontificio Instituto di Archeologia Christiana; New York: New York University Press, 1959); Asher Ovadiah, *Corpus of the Byzantine Churches in the Holy Land*, Translated by Rose Kirson (Bonn: Peter Hanstein Verlag, 1970); Asher Ovadiah and Carla Gomez de Silva, "Supplementum to the Corpus of the Byzantine Churches in the Holy Land," *Levant* 13 (1981): 200-261, 14 (1982): 1222-70, 16 (1984): 129-65.

5 Based on epigraphic evidence, Leah Di Segni says that we know of four civil basilicas erected in Palestine between the 4th and 7th centuries: Caesarea, Sepphoris, and two in Beth Shean. Compare that with some 112 churches built during the same period (not all of these were basilicas, however; see note 4 above); "Epigraphic documentation on building in the provinces of *Palaestina* and *Arabia*, 4th-7th c.," in *The Roman and Byzantine Near East*, Vol. 2, *Some Recent Ar4chaeological Research*, ed. J. H. Humphrey (Portsmouth, Rhode Island: Journal of Roman Archaeology, 1999), 157, 163.

colonnades displayed the majesty of both Caesar and Rome, but the activities it housed were mundane in comparison. By contrast, as we see in the travel diary of the fourth century nun Egeria, Christian basilicas accommodated a solemn and elaborate liturgy.[6] Christianity thus brought to the basilica a stately ritual that matched the building's regal architecture. Since the Christian basilica was the first public Christian building, we want to know why Christians chose a secular structure rather than some other structure, such as a temple, or one of their own invention.

Second, we must explain why Christians began erecting public buildings only in the fourth century. This is a problem because, with the advent of the Christian basilica, Christian worship was no longer conducted privately or in secret, admitting only the fully initiated and catechumens (potential converts), while excluding catechumens from the mass proper. The liturgy now was transformed into a public spectacle, accessible to all,[7] much as the worship of the Olympian pantheon had been.[8] Thus in the fourth century,

---

6 See the discussion in Chapter 4 below.

7 Egeria makes no mention of two services in the Jerusalem churches, a fore-mass that admitted catechumens, and the mass proper, which excluded them. Rather, her language implies that an undifferentiated congregation of worshipers gathered at appointed times in the various churches. See Chapter 4 below.

8 For the first 350 years of Christianity, worshipers gathered in homes or modest, privately owned structures—either houses or shops—that they converted for church use. The New Testament contains many references to Christians gathering in homes, some of which explicitly mention "the church in your house": Philem. 1-2; Rom. 16:5; Col. 4:15; see also Acts 2:46; 5:42; 12:12-16; 20:7-12, II Jn. 10. Likewise, the *Didache*, Ignatius, Justin Martyr, Tertullian, and many other early Christian works contain references to Christians gathering in various "places," which we assume to refer to private homes. For a complete catalogue of these mentions, with original text and translation, see Michael White, *Christian Architecture*, vol. II, 33-120. In these cases, one could not distinguish a

through its architecture and liturgy, Christianity recast itself as a public religion.

Third, we must explain why Christians continued to build their large, monumental churches only as basilicas rather than in a variety of architectural styles. That is, not only did Christians choose to build basilicas in the fourth century, but nearly all monumental churches built in the fourth through sixth centuries took basilical form.[9] Constantine erected the first in the Empire, so far as we know—Rome's basilica church of St. John the Lateran in 313—and soon other communities across the Empire began constructing their own.[10] We want to know why, when many different types of buildings could house large congregations, Christians built only one type of building.

---

church by its façade: church buildings looked exactly like the other homes in the neighborhoods in which they stood. By contrast, the first Christian basilicas were massive, magnificently decorated edifices constructed by the state. The first public Christian buildings thus were some of the most prominent in their cities, for they took over the civil basilica's architectural style, its grand size, and ostentatious display. Eusebius does say that at the end of the third century, between 258 (Cyprian's death) and 303 (Diocletian's first edict), Christians built large churches (εὐρεάς εἰς πλάτος...ἐκκλησίας; *HE* VIII.1.5), but his language is vague, and the archaeological record has not yet revealed any substantial church buildings from this time.

9 While many memorial churches were octagonal, cross-shaped, or circular (some of Constantine's basilicas incorporate these architectural features into their design; see the churches of the Holy Sepulcher and Holy Nativity, Figures 3 and 4 respectively), and many small churches were "chapels" or small halls, nearly all monumental churches took basilical form.

10 For example, in Palestine alone, before the fourth century we have archaeological remains of only one church: the house church at Capernaum. By contrast, in 1970 Asher Ovadiah catalogued 45 fourth and fifth century Palestinian churches, 34 (76 percent) of them basilicas; Asher Ovadiah, *Corpus of the Byzantine Churches*, Table no. 1.

Fourth, the floor plans of Constantine's basilicas all follow a standardized design.[11] We can identify Christian basilicas by a particular plan, common to all, that civil basilicas did not share. We may conclude, therefore, that Christian basilicas served a specific purpose, that is they symbolized a particular idea, or were meant to accommodate a particular behavior. For rather than reproducing the variety of basilicas that had existed before, Christians made only one type of basilica.[12] We want to know what happened in Christian basilicas—that did not happened in civil basilicas—that caused Christians to standardize their design.

Thus we naturally ask why the Christian basilica emerged. Given its abrupt appearance and immediate standardization, the Christian basilica appears to have been designed for a purpose. If this is so, what we want to know is, [1] for what purpose Christians used basilicas (that is, what happened in Christian basilicas), [2] why they adopted the basilical style for their churches, and [3] why they standardized their design.

In this study I aim to propose a hypothesis to answer these questions. As for what purpose Christians used basilicas (or what happened in them), I hypothesize that the answer is implicit in their design. That is, as with other Roman public buildings, the standardization of the Christian basilica's plan implies that it was designed to accommodate the movement of people within its structure. That is to say, the Christian basilica looks as if it was meant to encourage

---

11 We will unpack the features of this design more fully in Chapter 2 below.

12 As we shall see in Chapter 2, I do not claim that all Christian basilicas of the fourth century and following were identical, nor do I think that basilicas never deviated from the standard design that I claim they followed. Rather, I argue that Constantine's basilicas follow a design that subsequent basilicas emulate. Deviations from this design are infrequent enough for me to claim that they are exceptions to the rule.

behavior of a particular sort. If this is so, then by looking at Christian basilicas we ought to be able to infer what happened in them, much as we can infer from the plans of Roman theaters what sorts of things happened in them. We can tell, for instance, that people entered a theater through many vomitoria, and sat in curved and tiered rows, all facing toward a platform, apparently to observe what happened there. My first task, therefore, is to form a preliminary hypothesis that answers the question, What sort of movement did Christian basilicas accommodate? Answering that question should also suffice to answer why Christians adopted the basilical form, and why they standardized their design.

At the beginning of Chapter 2 I will spell out my hypothesis. Here it suffices to review the data that we will use in this study.

The Data for the Present Study

To link the data to the study, I must first state two assumptions. First, I assume that the key to understanding the design of Christian basilicas lies in describing the movement that took place in them. A second assumption is that the design of the Christian basilica itself yields a clue as to what movement it accommodated. In line with these two premises, the data that we require are as follows.

First, in Chapter 2 we will examine the floor plans of civil basilicas built before the fourth century, then I will lay out in more detail the standard design of Christian basilicas mentioned above. Based on a comparison and contrast of these two types, we will be able to infer what sort of activities or movement the Christian basilicas were designed to accommodate.

Our data will be the floor plans of Constantine's five extant basilicas. We examine only these five—the Lateran and St. Peter's (both in Rome), Holy Sepulcher (Jerusalem), Holy Nativity (Bethlehem), and Eleona (Mt. of Olives)[13] for the simple reason that each was commissioned by the same Emperor within 23 years of the others, between the construction of the Lateran in 313 and the Holy Sepulcher in 335, two years before Constantine's death. Thus, if the Christian basilica was designed from the outset to accommodate a certain type of ritual movement, this fact should explain the design of all of Constantine's basilicas. I restrict the study to those, excluding others, because it is possible that those who designed other Christian basilicas simply copied Constantine's without understanding what those buildings were designed to do.[14]

In Chapter 3 I will compare the emergence of the Christian basilica, as I think it happened, with evidence presented by two other sets of data: Christian art and the language of Christian authors. By "Christian art" I mean carvings in stone sarcophagi and ivory and wooden panels that depict biblical or early Christian themes. My sample of objects does not include frescos, textiles, or metals except for one coin. By "the language of Christian authors" I mean those writers of the first through fourth centuries (Paul, Justin Martyr, Theophilus, Appolonius, Irenaeus, Ambrose, Chrysostom, Eusebius, and others) who both instruct

---

13 A sixth, Constantine's so-called basilica at Mamre near Hebron, may not be a basilica at all; it is difficult to determine its specific floor plan; see A.E. Mader, "Les fouilles allemandes au Ramet El Khalil: la Mambré biblique de la tradition primitive," in *Revue Biblique* 39 (1930) 84: 115-7; Figs. 2, 5; Pls. 5, 7. A seventh, the basilica at Tyre, which Eusebius discusses, has not been discovered. Scholars dispute whether an eighth, Hagia Sophia in Constantinople, was begun under Constantine.

14 I do not think that this is so, however, for basilicas across the Empire do not reintroduce the variety of basilical plans found in the civil basilica. It seems to me that we cannot explain this fact by means of aesthetics alone.

Christians in the faith and defend Christianity to the Emperor. Why do I look at these two media? I wish to argue that the appearance of the Christian basilica reflects the new status of Christianity as a licit religion in the fourth century. If it does, then I wish to know if other media reflect this status as well. Thus I ask if Christian art and literature also present abrupt new forms as counterparts to the appearance of the Christian basilica, or if Christian architecture alone presents new designs and new ideas.

Having inferred from their design what movement the Christian basilica was designed to accommodate, in Chapter 4 I will search for references to these activities in the fourth century or earlier.

In Chapter 5 I will compare Constantine's basilicas with a control group: early synagogue buildings. I wish to determine if Jewish basilicas recapitulate the design of Christian basilicas, or if the movement or location of people in the Jewish liturgy after 70 C.E. produced its own architectural plan.

Prior Solutions to the Problem

Before I announce my hypothesis, let me review previous work in the field of early Christian architecture. Two primary schools of thought aim to account for the emergence of the Christian basilica in the fourth century. The first (in the order in which we treat them, not the chronological order of their formulation) argues that church architecture develops in linear progression, beginning with the first century house church recorded in the New Testament and "naturally" evolving to the basilica in the fourth century. Michael White, who has written a two-volume comprehensive treatment of archaeological, textual, and epigraphic sources,[15] sees the predecessor of the basilica in the house atria and the elongated halls of the late third and early fourth century, such as the early church under San Crisogono in Rome (Fig. 1). White asserts that church architecture develops from the first century New Testament house church to the fourth century basilica in increments, including as intermediate steps the modified *domus ecclesiae* (a house with enlarged interior space to facilitate Christian gatherings), and *aulus ecclesiae* (a former house or other building, completely taken over and modified as a church).

White solves the problem of the Christian basilica's origin by placing it at the end of an evolutionary process. Thus he does not ask why Christians chose to build churches as basilicas to begin with, or why they continued to build them for many centuries. These simply are not issues in an evolutionary model, for one can explain every step as "natural".[16] This is an odd formulation, for it characterizes deliberate human acts as natural events, or accidents. But this is not what happened at all in the development of church architecture: when, for example, the house churches at Dura Europos and Capernaum no longer served the needs of growing congregations, they knocked down walls, and at Dura they installed a baptistry. In other places they built small churches from the ground up. These are not examples of "natural" evolution, but of humans adapting their environments with forethought, a sense of aesthetics, and, we assume, expressing an ethos.

---

15 Michael L. White, *The Social Origins of Christian Architecture*, 2 vols. (Valley Forge, PA: Trinity Press International, 1990-7). Another well-known scholar of church architecture, J.W. Crowfoot, describes the architecture of specific churches without analyzing the data; he does not tell us what it means; J.W. Crowfoot, *Early Churches in Palestine* (College Park: McGrath Publishing Company, 1971).

16 White's language: *Christian Architecture*, Vol. I, 128.

White's solution, therefore, cannot adequately account for the appearance of the church basilica. First, as stated above, Christian basilicas emerge practically overnight with the construction of the Lateran and its subsequent continuators and copiers. An evolutionary model, on the other hand, presupposes that things change in incremental steps; it cannot accommodate the sudden appearance of sophisticated new forms that have no precedent. Second, White's evolutionary model fails to account for how one species, and not many, filled an evolutionary niche. That is, the evolutionary model cannot explain the development of the basilica when many other architectural styles could also accommodate large congregations. We are left, in our case, to ask why Constantine and other Christians built large churches only as basilicas, if their sole need was to hold more people. That is, White has not explained how many types of church buildings "evolved" into one building.

In contrast to White, other scholars, represented here by Richard Krautheimer and J.B. Ward-Perkins, see no reason to look further than the civil basilica for the model of the Christian basilica.[17] Both see that the basilica's imposing size could house large numbers of worshippers, and both note that the spectacular adornment of the interiors of Constantine's basilicas, as well as the clothing of the Bishop himself, borrow directly from state ceremony.[18] It is here that we find our first hint that the grandness and glory of Constantine's basilicas reflect the Church's new status in the

---

17 Ward-Perkins, "Origins of the Christian Basilica," 85-7; Krautheimer, "Early Christian Architecture," 11ff.

18 Krautheimer, "Early Christian Architecture," 11-2, and *Christian and Byzantine Architecture*, 40; Ward-Perkins, "Origins of the Christian Basilica," 87; see also Beskow, *Rex Gloriae: The Kingship of Christ in the Early Church*, trans. Eric J. Sharpe (Stockholm: Almqvist & Wiksells, 1962), 15.

imperial state, which lends an important step to our argument, as we shall see in Chapter 3.

Both scholars, however, stop short of accounting for why Constantine made the changes to the basilica form that he did. It is reasonable to assume that one of Constantine's goals was to admit large numbers of worshippers in a grand and ostentatious imperial style. While such a purpose might account for the structures' size, we are still at pains to understand why Constantine's monumental churches are *only* basilicas, and why they are all a *particular type* of basilica.

In 1934, S. Lang suggested that the predecessor for the Christian basilica lay neither in Christian architecture nor the civil basilica.[19] Rather, using the palaces at Spalato, Antiochia (as described in Libanius and Theodoret), and Thessalonike, he hypothesized a one-to-one correspondence between the Christian basilica and the imperial palace. The transept of the basilica represented the palace proper with its living quarters and audience hall, while the nave with its interior columniation represented the peristyle, the short colonnaded street that led to and stood at right angles to the palace.[20] Lang's hypothesis, however, proved difficult because, of Constantine's original six basilicas that have been uncovered, only St. Peter's had a transept. In a footnote added after his paper had gone to press Lang reveals that he learned too late of Krautheimer's discovery that the Lateran had no transept.[21] Lang's work is problematic for another reason as well: although he theorized about connections between the Emperor and early Christian conceptions of Christ, he did not demonstrate that the liturgical movement

---

19 S. Lang, "A few suggestions toward a new solution of the origin of the early christian basilica," *Rivista di archeologia christiana* 30 (1934): 189-208.

20 S. Lang, "The origin of the early christian basilica," 201-3.

21 Ibid., 206, n. 84

that took place in the earliest Christian basilicas found any match in the activities of the imperial palace. He does present one idea of interest to the thesis presented here: the arrangement of the nave and side aisles of the Christian basilica resembles the layout of the colonnaded thoroughfare with its street and sidewalks. The present work will provide evidence for that comparison.

In conclusion, none of the scholars surveyed here contemplates how the design of the Christian basilica may accommodate the movement of people. If we can answer that question, the answer to why Christians built basilicas in the first place, and secondly, why the built them the way that they did, should follow. Turning now to the body of the argument, the next step is to examine the architectural features that make a building a basilica, as well as those that make a basilica a church.

Chapter 2.
The Standardization of Christian Basilicas

In this chapter I aim to lay out the data that leads me to formulate a hypothesis that explains the design of Constantine's basilicas. Specifically, I will show that Constantine's basilicas represent a particular *type* of basilica; they have features found here and there in civil basilicas around the Empire, but of these, only Constantine's were constructed within so short a time frame and commissioned by one Emperor. We justifiably, therefore, may call the design of Constantine's basilicas "standardized." The task in this chapter is to spell out this design, then to craft a hypothesis that accounts for it.

Roman Civil Basilicas and Constantine's Basilicas

Krautheimer has suggested that the first church basilicas constructed in the fourth century C.E. were new creations, variations on the older theme of Rome's civil basilicas.[22] He lists the standard features of early Christian basilicas that allow them to be classified as basilicas, and also makes note of those features that are unique to Constantine's. We register Krautheimer's observations and make some additions.

First, the literary evidence demonstrates that the new monumental churches constructed after the Edict of Milan (313 C.E.) are recognized as basilicas from the outset, suggesting that they did not "evolve" from some other structure, such as the house atrium or *domus ecclesiae*. For example, Constantine himself (as recorded by Eusebius)

22 Krautheimer, "Early Christian Architecture," 14-5.

instructs Macarius, Bishop of Jerusalem, to build his church near the cave of Christ's tomb as "a basilica better than those everywhere,"[23] and Eusebius refers to the Holy Sepulcher with the same language.[24] In 333 the Bordeaux Pilgrim also calls the Holy Sepulcher a "basilica," which he then qualifies with the language, "that is, a house of the Lord".[25] Following the Pilgrim in 384, Egeria calls the "great church" attached to the Anastasis of the Holy Sepulcher a "basilica,"[26] although she uses the same word for the Anastasis itself.[27]

Notice that in these passages the term "basilica" is fluid in its usage. We cannot, for instance, tell if the other basilicas Constantine mentions ("those everywhere") are church basilicas or civil basilicas. Likewise, the Bordeaux Pilgrim must qualify what he means by the term, presumably because civil basilicas are still in use. Egeria seems to call any grand building with interior columniation a "basilica," even the rotunda of the Anastasis. Nevertheless, even within the term's broad sense, its usage is restricted to a particular architectural type, or to other buildings that serve the same purpose as a Christian basilica. Apparently Krautheimer is correct when he says, "Everyone knew what a basilica was."[28]

---

23 βασιλικὴν τῶν ἀπανταχοῦ βελτίονα; Eusebius, *VC*, III.31 (*PG* 20, 1091).

24 ὁ βασίλειος συνῆπτο νεὼς; Ibid., III.36 (*PG* 20, 1096); cf. III.37 (*PG* 20, 1097).

25 *iusso Constantini imperatoris basilica facta est, id est dominicum*; *It. Burd.*, 594 (Geyer, 23).

26 *in basilica, quae est loco iuxta Anastasium*; S. Siluae, *Pereg.* 24.8 (Geyer, 73).

27 *tota basilica Anastasis*; ibid., 24.10.

28 "Early Christian Architecture," 14. It should be noted that Eusebius most often refers to the new magnificent edifices erected under Constantine primarily as "temples" (νεώς) and "houses of prayer" (προσευκτηρίων): *HE*, X.2.1, 3.1; he also refers to the monumental

Second, the churches are recognizable as basilicas by several regular features (Figs. 2-14). Both civil and church basilicas are elongated halls in which rows of interior columns partition a central mall or nave from two or more side aisles. A two-story high ceiling, often with exposed roof timbers (Figs. 7, 11), rises over the nave, while lower, single-story ceilings cover the aisles. Clerestories over the nave illuminate both the nave and the opposite aisles. Both civil and Constantinian basilicas typically have at least one apse.

So Byzantine church basilicas are recognizable as basilicas because of several standardized features: a nave with side aisles, interior columniation, clerestory illumination, and the presence of an apse. On the other hand, Constantine's basilicas do not recapitulate the diversity of civil basilical forms. Rather, the differences between the two types of structures define a standardized style for later church basilicas that persists in spite of the variations—usually in size—that these basilicas begin to display.

1. Civil basilicas frequently stand adjacent to the forum, per Vitruvius' prescription that they accommodate the forum's commerce in inclement weather (see, for example, Fig. 13).[29] By contrast, only Constantine's Holy Sepulcher in Jerusalem stands near the forum,[30] although the proximity of

---

church at Tyre as "a royal house" (βασίλειον οἶκον): *HE*, X.4.44. Oddly, Leah Di Segni has noticed that despite the use of βασιλική in literary sources of the 4th century, no church built in Palestine in the 4th through 7th centuries is called a "basilica" in its dedicatory inscription. Di Segni, "Epigraphic evidence for building in *Palaestina* and *Arabia* (4th-7th c.)," 157.

29 Vitruvius, *The Ten Books on Architecture*, trans. Morris Hicky Morgan (New York: Dover Publications, 1960) [originally published in 1914], 132; for an example, see plans of Lepcis Magna forum and Timgad, Figures 13 and 16 in this thesis.

30 Eusebius, *VC* III.39 (*PG* 20, 1100); cf. S. Siluae, *Pereg.* 43.7 (Geyer, 95).

the cave of the sepulcher to the market clearly is accidental. Krautheimer, in fact, argues that the early Christian basilicas incorporate the forum into their design by attaching porticoed courtyards to the sides having the main entrance,[31] as is the case with all of Constantine's basilicas treated in this book.

2. Whereas civil basilicas typically place two apses opposite each other in the short walls (Figs. 8, 13), place one in a long wall (Fig. 10), or have no apse at all (Fig. 9),[32] Constantine's basilicas uniformly place only one apse in the short wall opposite the main entrance. The sole exception to this rule is the church of the Holy Nativity in Bethlehem, which has no apse. In its place an entrance lets into the octagonal hall over the cave of the nativity (Fig. 5). Palestinian churches locate their apses in the eastern wall, except for the Holy Sepulcher, whose apse is in the western wall toward the sepulcher (Fig. 4),[33] while the Roman churches have theirs in the western wall. In either case, nearly all later church basilicas across the Empire maintain this east-west orientation.

3. Similarly, whereas civil basilicas could have their main entrance in any wall, usually the long wall adjacent to the forum,[34] the primary entrance to Constantine's basilicas is

---

31 Krautheimer, "Early Christian Architecture," 15.

32 In Vitruvius' basilica at Fano the apse contains curved benches for the Tribunal.

33 Vincent's plan and stone-by-stone drawing of the Eleona church provides no north arrow. I assume that this means that the apse is in the east; "L'église de l'Eléona," *Revue Biblique* 20 (1911): 259, Fig. 10 [Fig. 6 in this book], Planche 1.

34 Ward-Perkins argues that basilicas in the East typically are of the "long" type, with entrances in one short end opposite an apse or tribunal in the other, while in the West they are "broad," the entrance and apse/tribunal opposite each other in the long walls; "Origins of the Christian Basilica," 76-7.

always in the short wall opposite the apse and frequently is tri-portal.[35]

4. Constantine's basilicas uniformly have no aisles parallel to the short walls; the aisles run only parallel to the nave.

5. Constantine's basilicas have no shops or offices lining the aisles, nor second story offices above the aisles, as civil basilicas often do.[36]

6. I note with some caution the so-called "triumphal arch" at the terminus of the nave, between the altar and the apse, mentioned by Ward-Perkins in conjunction with the Lateran and St. Peter's.[37]

As mentioned in Chapter 1, all of these features, which distinguish Constantine's basilicas from civil basilicas, uniformly persist, with exceptions here and there, in church basilicas through the seventh century and even up to the present. Thus I claim that the plan of Constantine's churches is "standardized," and I suggest these churches were designed for a purpose. That is, both the uniformity and longevity of this design indicate that Constantinian basilicas are not simply aesthetic variations on the older theme of Roman architecture. Otherwise we might see later Christian basilicas returning to a "broad" type, or completely surrounding the nave with aisles, or placing the altar elsewhere than in front of

---

35 The 19th c. plan of Old St. Peter's shows a tri-portal entrance opening into the nave while two flanking entrances let into the adjacent aisles, making five entrances (Fig. 2); Corbo's plan of the Holy Sepulcher (Fig. 4), Richmond's of the Holy Nativity (Fig. 5), and Vincent's of Eleona (Fig.6) all reconstruct tri-portal entrances into the nave and side aisles.

36 Krautheimer says that the cornice of St. Peter's apparently supported a railing that allowed foot traffic on all four sides of the nave, but this is clearly not even a secondary area of traffic for the building; "Early Christian Architecture," 15; see Fig. 2, p. 377.

37 Ward-Perkins, "Origins of the Christian Basilica," 85; cf. S. Lang, "The origin of the early christian basilica," 208.

the apse and opposite the entrance. The fact that the plan of Christian basilicas is standardized means that the need to accommodate large congregations cannot fully explain why Constantine's grand churches are only basilicas, and why the basilica immediately became the preferred architectural style for monumental churches.

How can we account for both the diversity of civil basilicas, and the uniformity of Constantinian and all subsequent Christian basilicas? To answer that question, we begin with the assumption that these basilicas accommodate a specific type of new behavior, not found in, or not emphasized in, civil basilicas. Furthermore, it is possible that Constantine's basilicas mimic another structure that already accommodated that kind of behavior.

This type of architectural adaptation finds its match in the present century, where a Christian structure adopted features of a secular building that was designed to house, not just a crowd, but an assembly of people engaged in a particular behavior. Many church sanctuaries have for some years contained raised platforms resembling theater or auditorium stages. Recently, however, some sanctuaries have adopted additional characteristics of auditoriums, including sloping or tiered floors toward the stage, theater benches with folding seats, and curved or angled rows so that every seat directly faces the podium or stage.

These changes are not simply cosmetic, but accommodate a specific worship style. It is not the movement of people down the axis of the sanctuary that is encouraged by these structures, but clear sight lines and acoustics, giving all worshipers visual and auditory access to the performance of the service.[38] Thus as the aim of worship

---

38 Peter Hammond, *Liturgy and Architecture* (New York: Columbia University Press, 1961), 1-11; Pls. 6, 10, 23, 25, 47, 50, 52 in Ch. 6; Plns. 2-6, 10 in Ch. 6. See also the discussion in James and Susan White, *Church*

more and more approximates the aim of public performances of various types, so the architecture of the one mimics the architecture of the other. Incidentally, many Protestant liturgies have no processional (except for special occasions, such as weddings and funerals), and the sanctuaries in those traditions that have no processional also typically have no central aisle between the pews. This is an important correlation to note, as we shall see presently.

To apply the above analogy to Constantine's basilicas, what activities may we infer happened in them? Removing the aisles at the short ends, and placing the apse and altar at the short end opposite the entrance, implies that these buildings are constructed to accommodate or encourage two-way traffic flow. Celebrants come in the main entrance, and move straight ahead toward the altar in front of the apse opposite that entrance. To exit they reverse course, moving down the nave, away from the apse and altar, and exit through the same doors by which they entered. Figures 11 and 12 illustrate how the standardized design of Constantine's basilicas encourages two-way traffic flow, which is uncommon in most civil basilicas, whose encircling aisles and surrounding shops seem to encourage traffic in all directions, much like the forum itself. Although the tribunal and/or the apse—frequently containing an effigy of the Emperor—provide a focal point in these structures, the architecture does not invite foot traffic to begin at one end of the building and terminate at the other. Ward-Perkins' "long" type civil basilicas in the East may be an exception, for he describes them as having "longitudinal colonnades running without a break from entrance to *tribunal*," although he names only two examples, the Caesareum at Cyrene and the Hadrianic basilica

---

Architecture: Building and Renovating for Christian Worship (Nashville: Abingdon, 1988), 18-37, 50-53.

at Kremna, Pisidia.[39] His three illustrations of long-type basilicas—Pompeii, Corinth, and Lepcis Magna—all surround the nave with aisles.[40]

Here we make special note of the large public peristyle building at Sepphoris, Israel, currently under excavation by J. F. Strange (Fig. 14). This two-story, 60 x 40 meter basilical structure, which takes up an entire city block, was constructed in the early first century and substantially remodeled in the late third or early fourth. Strange is inclined to interpret the last use of the building as a market because of the number of coins and the type of pottery and glass found on the floors and in the drains. On the white mosaic floors, black stripes apparently direct traffic, not down the nave, but around the sides, where shops line the aisles.[41] Furthermore, although there are indications that a tri-portal entrance may offer access to the building from the courtyard to the east, in the long southern wall another large entrance (measuring 2.1 meters) lets into the southern aisle near the eastern wall that partitions the basilica from the portico. Four other smaller doors (1.77 meters wide) pierce this same wall to the west of the large entrance, and Strange has located at least one similar entrance in the long northern wall opposite.[42] Apparently the mosaic floor and location of the doors encourage explicitly what the architectural style itself invites implicitly: traffic around the periphery of the structure.

---

39 Krautheimer, "Early Christian Achitecture," 77.

40 Ibid., 73, Fig. 2.

41 James F. Strange, "The Eastern Basilical Building," in *Sepphoris in Galilee: Crosscurrents in Culture*, ed. Rebecca Nagy *et al.* (North Carolina Museum of Art, 1996), 117-121.

42 James F. Strange, telephone conversation with the author (Tampa, FL, June, 1999).

The Roman Thoroughfare

Hence the architecture of civil basilicas appears to invite all-way or circular pedestrian traffic, between offices and shops, within and across the nave. In this way, basilicas imitate the design of the porticoed forum, whose purpose they served in bad weather.[43] By the same token, the fact that Constantine's (and, to reiterate, nearly all subsequent Christian basilicas) standardize a basilical design with only longitudinal aisles parallel to the nave and the main entrance in the short wall opposite the apse, suggests that it is no longer all-way traffic that these structures accommodate, but two-way traffic.

Having reached this inference, it is striking that the grand Roman structure that accommodates large volumes of primarily two-way traffic, the thoroughfare street, also has a wide central avenue bounded by colonnaded porches or sidewalks on two sides. Figure 13 is a photo of the main avenue in Timgad,[44] while Figure 16 is the Arcadiané at Ephesus. The parallels between them and a Christian basilica's floor plan are arresting. The tri-portal triumphal arch near the west gate of Timgad only enhances the similarities.

Notice that the traffic on the thoroughfare falls into two different types. During the course of a normal day people travel both the paved street itself and the sidewalks to destinations within and without the city, and to the shops and offices lining the boulevard. Pedestrians may walk on the street

---

43 This fact may strengthen the argument that the name "basilica"— βασιλική—originated as an adjective, as in the "royal porch"—στοὰ βασιλική—in Athens. See Ward-Perkins, "Origins of the Christian Basilica," 70.

44 From William L. MacDonald, *the Architecture of the Roman Empire, Vol. II: An Urban Appraisal* (New Haven and London: Yale University Press, 1986), 28.

street as well as the sidewalks, for they need not hurry to avoid the ox or equine-drawn carts. On special occasions, however, pedestrians must confine themselves to the sidewalks to make way for processionals, primarily triumphal military parades and *adventi* of important state officials, which we will examine more fully below.

It is the latter pomp that concerns us here. As noted, it is striking that the *cardo*,[45] with its wide avenue, colonnaded sidewalks, and state parades, finds its architectural match in the Constantinian basilica, with its wide nave, colonnaded side aisles, and—I presume—solemn processionals.

The task before us now takes its shape. We have noted the architectural similarities between major thoroughfares and Constantinian basilicas, which we can plainly see, and their parallel functions, which we presume to exist. What is required now is data that will allow us to hypothesize that these similarities are not accidental, but intentional.

Before moving on, therefore, Table 1 compares the widths of major thoroughfares in cities across the Roman Empire with the widths of Constantine's basilicas.

---

45 The *cardo maximus* is the north-south "main street" that runs through the center of town, usually to the forum.

Table 1. Comparison: Constantinian Basilicas (width of nave) with Roman Thoroughfares (width of street)

Constantinian Basilicas		Roman Thoroughfares[46]	
Lateran	25.1 m[47]	Antioch	29 m
St. Peter's	apr. 23.5 m[48]	Gerasa	22/24 m
		Rome, Via Flaminia	21 m
		Apamea	23 m
		Ephesus, Arcadiané	23 m
Holy Sepulcher	14 m[49]	Augst, NW-SE	14 m
		Pompeii, NE-SW	7/14 m
Holy Nativity	10.4 m[50]	Ostia	8/10 m
Eleona	11 m[51]		

Table 1 verifies that Constantine's basilicas are neither too wide nor too narrow to be modeled after the thoroughfare. Rather, both the standardized style and the

46 From MacDonald, *Architecture of the Roman Empire, Vol. II*, 41-2. Because MacDonald does not say, I must assume that his dimensions are of the width of the street itself, not including the sidewalks.

47 Richard Krautheimer, "The Constantinian Basilica of the Lateran," in *Early Christian, Medieval, and Renaissance Art* (New York: New York University Press, 1969), 22, Text fig. 5.

48 Krautheimer, *Christian and Byzantine Architecture*, 55, Fig. 22.

49 Virgilio C. Corbo, *Il Santo Sepolcro di Gerusalemme*, Parte II (Jerusalem: Franciscan Printing Press, 1981), Pl. 3.

50 Asher Ovadiah, *Corpus of the Byzantine Churches in the Holy Land*, trans. Rose Kirson (Bonn: Peter Hanstein Verlag, 1970), 34.

51 Ibid., 82.

dimensions of Constantinian churches match the appearance and size of major Roman streets. This is the first piece of concrete evidence that supports the hypothesis that Constantine's basilicas were designed to accommodate a processional, which itself was modeled after Roman imperial processionals.

That hypothesis, as I have laid it out, assumes that in the fourth century Christian architecture reflects the new relationship between the Church and the Roman state that began with Constantine's edict of 313. To test that assumption, in the next chapter I ask if this relationship is expressed in other media besides architecture.

Chapter 3.
Church and State in the Fourth Century

Having formulated a hypothesis that accounts for the standardization of Constantine's basilicas, I now aim to strengthen it through supporting evidence. Specifically, I have speculated about how the relationship between Church and state in the fourth century is worked out in one public medium: architecture. In this chapter I will review how Christianity worked out that same relationship in other media, namely literature and art. My intent is to show that in the fourth century Christianity recast itself as a public religion, and this shift is visible in many different media.

The Kingship of Christ and the Divinity of the Emperor

The Church in the fourth century began to reflect its status, both as a newly state-sanctioned religion, and as the religion favored by the Emperor himself. As evidence for this, first, as I argued in Chapter 1, Constantine ordered the construction of eight magnificent Christian basilicas, an architectural style that formerly was reserved for civil structures that reflected the power of the Emperor and his tribunal.

Second, beginning in the fourth century, the Church's royal titles for Christ no longer set it in opposition to the state, but were accepted by the state. Deissmann, Setton, MacCormack, Beskow,[52] and others have well explored the

---

52 Adolf Deissmann, *Light from the Ancient East: The New Testament Illustrated by Recently Discovered Texts of the Graeco-Roman World*, revised, trans. Lionel R.M. Strachan (Grand Rapids: Baker Books House, 1980 [German, 1909]); Kenneth M. Setton, *Christian Attitude Towards the Emperor in the*

link between the early Christian liturgy and the Emperor cult, and the shift in Christian attitudes in the fourth century. These scholars have established the correlation between titles for both Christ and Caesar, although there remains debate—and rightly so—about the nature of the link. As to the titles shared by both cults, Deissmann argued that the common usage is coincidental, since the Church derived much of its theological language from the Septuagint, and therefore did not take over imperial language from the state. However, although the coincidence of imperial titles initially is accidental, it quickly became polemical, according to Deissmann. Even as early as Paul[53] the Church asserted that while the Emperor may have been king (βασιλεύς), he was not king of kings (βασιλεὺς βασιλέων), God (θεός), Son of God (θέου υἱός), Lord (κύριος), Savior (σωτήρ), or High Priest (ἀρχιερεύς or Pontifex Maximus).[54] For the Christian, whose attitudes toward the Emperor were spelled out by Paul,[55] Justin Martyr,[56] Theophilus,[57] Appolonius,[58] Irenaeus,[59] Chrysostom[60] and others, Caesar ruled by divine authority, but Christ alone was divine.[61] Christian use of this

---

Fourth Century, Especially As Shown in Addresses to the Emperor (New York: AMS Press, 1967); Per Beskow, *Rex Gloriae, op. cit.*; Sabine MacCormack, *Art and Ceremony in Late Antiquity* (Berkeley, U. of California Press, 1981); see also Lily Ross Taylor, *The Divinity of the Roman Emperor* (Middletown, CT: American Philological Association, 1931); Daniel N. Schowalter, *The Emperor and the Gods: Images from the Time of Trajan* (Minneapolis: Fortress Press, 1993).

53 II Thess. 2:4; Deissmann, *Light from the East*, 343.

54 Ibid., 342-66; cf. Setton, *Christian Attitude*, 18.

55 Rom. 13:1-7.

56 *Apol. I.*

57 *Ad Autolycum.*

58 *Acts.*

59 *Adv. Haer.*

60 *Hom. de stat. VII.*

61 Although for an example of enmity toward the Emperor, see

language, says Deissmann, marks "a polemical parallelism between the cult of the Emperor and the cult of Christ, which makes itself felt where ancient words derived by Christianity from the treasury of the Septuagint and the Gospels happen to coincide with solemn concepts of the Imperial cult which sounded the same or similar."[62]

Setton, by contrast, argues that by the fourth century, the relationship between the Church and the state could no longer be characterized as polemical.[63] He shows that after the ascendancy of Christianity in the fourth century, panegyrists continue to deify Emperors with their language,[64] while "the most Christian Emperor Theodosius appears to have heard himself called a God with no less pleasure than Maximian, persecutor of Christians."[65] For example, Eusebius' well-known panegyric, *In Praise of Constantine*, from start to finish uses both imperial language for God and divine language for the Emperor "to indicate their close resemblance one to the other."[66]

Beskow spells out the new problems that these legitimate and sometimes competing claims for divinity and kingship caused between Church and state. Specifically, after Constantine Christians were forced to deal with the problem of how to accommodate the Emperor into the Church. The Empire now had two kings, Christ and Caesar, and it struggled to resolve the issue of whether Caesar ruled the Church as he did the Empire, or if he fell under the church's authority. According to Beskow, who draws his discussion

---

Hippolytus *De Antichr., Comm. on Dan.*

62 Deissmann, *Light from the East*, 342.

63 Note that he mistakenly accuses Deissmann of deriving "the characteristic language of primitive Christianity from the Emperor-cult," Setton, *Christian Attitude*, 18 n. 7.

64 Ibid., 30.

65 Ibid., 29.

66 Ibid., 47.

from the works of Ambrose (*Sermo c. Auxent*) and Chrysostom (*Hom. de stat.*), in working out this problem the Church emphasized the priesthood of Christ rather than his kingship, and it gave priority and authority to the former. It is a short step from there to claim that the bishop himself has authority over the Emperor.[67]

This type of theological and political dilemma is very different from the problem that occupied Christian writers before the peace of Constantine. Then, as we have said, there were Christians who advocated obedience to Caesar and those who called him Antichrist. Beskow says that Hippolytus, who stands out as an example of the latter, argues, "one of the signs of the Antichrist is his faithful imitation of Christ in all things. The kingdom of Antichrist is thus a shameless copy of the Kingdom of Christ."[68] Before the peace of Constantine, therefore, at least some Christians preached an anti-Empire sentiment that saw the earthly kingdom as heaven's shadow, as its dark counterfeit. After Constantine, the Church faced the problem of how to require obedience to Caesar while placing him under Christ's authority.

The scholarship covered here shows the shift in Christian attitudes toward the state that happened in the fourth century. By the fourth century and later, Christian language about the Emperor, which previously had ranged from positive to ambivalent to polemical, now existed more or less comfortably side-by-side with panegyrics, at least for some Christian writers. No longer were Christian spokesmen (e.g. Apollonius) composing apologies to the Emperor that explained why, while Christians would pray for him, they would neither worship him nor call him "Lord." Now God had bestowed upon the Emperor divine wisdom, and the

---

67 Beskow, *Rex Gloriae*, 328; cf. 322-3.

68 Ibid., 177; Hippolytus, *De Anichr.* 6.

Empire itself reflected the power of heaven. That is, not only did God rule from on high *through* the Emperor, but in contrast with the picture of "the kingdom of Antichrist" painted by Hippolytus, the Empire was now an imitation of heaven itself. As Setton says, "Truly God had been cast in the image of the Roman Emperor."[69]

We may speculate that the fourth century Church—having quickly moved from illicit to licit state religion—now used these parallelisms between Christ and Caesar to legitimize its newfound power. The Church no longer needed to protest worship of the Emperor, but could now praise him, if not as a divine being, then as a divine appointee. Nowhere is this clearer than in *In Praise of Constantine*, where Eusebius beatifies the Emperor as the Church's benefactor and champion.

This panegyric clears the way for Christian worship, which was already using much of the language that the state reserved for the Emperor, to appropriate the splendor of state architecture as well, especially if the churches in question were commissioned by the Emperor himself. Eusebius lays this transition out in his *Church History*, in which he describes both Constantine's edict requiring the return of Christian lands and buildings seized in Diocletian's pogrom, and the new church buildings that were constructed more glorious than before.[70] The *Church History* goes on to describe Constantine's church at Tyre, which, judging from Eusebius' language, may have been a magnificent basilica with an attached four-porticoed porch.[71] Likewise, *Life of Constantine* records the Emperor's orders (cited in Chapter 2 above) that the Holy Sepulcher should be a "basilica" surpassing all

69 Ibid., 48.

70 *HE* VIII.1.5-10.3.1 (*PG* 20, 740-848).

71 *HE* X.4.36-46 (*PG* 20, 864-8).

others in beauty.[72] In the fourth century, Christians recast Caesar as God's champion, and recast the basilica, formerly a house of civil law, as the house of God.

Imperial Symbols in Christian Art

Third, just as the imperial language of Christianity became legitimate in the fourth century while Christian architecture achieved imperial grandeur and proportions, we can also make a case that in the same period Christian art began to incorporate imperial motifs. Beskow argues that this did not begin until around 337, the time of Constantine's death, from which date the earliest so-called *Majestas* Christian images survive: a set of sarcophagi depicting "the Cross in the centre, crowned by the Constantinian *labarum* in a laurel wreath, and surrounded by the sun and moon, symbolizing the cosmic dimensions of salvation."[73] Notice, however, that Beskow is talking about stone carvings. Any earlier carvings in more perishable media, such as wood, showing both Christian and imperial emblems, are less likely to have survived 16 centuries. For example, a 1947 exhibition of early Christian and Byzantine art in Baltimore displayed 80 stone sculptures, 106 ivory and bone carvings, 149 bronzes, and 8 wood carvings.[74] Wood carvings thus made up 2.3% of the exhibition. If the number of artifacts collected for the exhibition is in any way proportional to the percentage of these materials that actually survived, then stone, bone, and bronze objects make up 43 times the number of surviving

---

72 *VC*, III, 31 (*PG* 20, 1091).

73 Beskow, *Rex Gloriae*, 22; for a photo of a similar sarcophagus showing a wreathed *chi-rho* over a cross with flanking scenes from the passion surmounted by victory wreaths, see Michael Gough, *The Origins of Christian Art* (NewYork: Praeger Publishers, 1973), 108-9, Pl. 91.

74 *Early Christian and Byzantine Art* (Baltimore: Trustees of the Walters Art Gallery, 1947), 23-79.

wood artifacts from the Byzantine era. Apparently, if there were any fourth century carvings in wood that depicted Christ as Caesar, they would not have endured.

Thus we can argue that not all of the data is in for Beskow to argue with such certitude. On the other hand, while the data may not allow us to ascribe any imperial themes to Christian art in Constantine's own time or earlier, we may attribute their appearance as a consequence of his reforms. That is, as we have discussed, the idea of Christ as king does not begin with Constantine's reforms, much less his death, but we may credibly infer that Christians' ability to represent imperial motifs in imperishable media without fear of reprisal—as well as the sanction to construct monumental Christian basilicas—begins in 313.

As evidence for imperial motifs in fourth-century Christian art I present three examples.

1. Beskow lists the above-mentioned sarcophagi, as well as others dating to around 360 C.E., [75] which represent Christ enthroned on heaven's vault—personified as *Coelus*—and handing the law to St. Peter. Grabar provides a photograph of one such sarcophagus, whose bottom panel shows Christ's entry into Jerusalem astride the donkey (Fig. 17). This sarcophagus bears a resemblance to a top panel on the Arch of Galerius at Thessalonika, which shows Galerius entering the city on a horse and being greeted by the citizens, while the bottom panel depicts Diocletian and Maximian enthroned over the personified sky and earth (Fig. 18).[76]

2. Beskow also mentions two mosaics, from around 360-370 C.E., in St. Costanza, the mausoleum of Constantine's daughter Constantina. One shows a purple-clad Christ enthroned on the world and handing Peter the keys of heaven; the other shows Christ standing with the apostles on

75 The date is from Gough, *Christian Art*, 107.

76 Ibid., Pl. 10.

the mount of Paradise, with his right hand raised and his left offering Peter a scroll that reads *Dominus pacem dat.*[77] These examples, says Beskow, adopt the motif of Caesar holding an *adlocutio* (a salutation) or giving over a *mandatum* (a commission).[78]

3. MacCormack prints a photograph of an ivory plaque that portrays the resurrected Christ ascending from the tomb and grasping the welcoming hand of God, which extends downward from a cloud (Fig. 19). This scene finds a match in the reverse of a coin that depicts the apotheosis of Constantine, who rises in a chariot and also reaches for the descending hand of God (Fig. 20).[79]

Beskow and MacCormack accept these three examples as straightforward representations of imperial motifs in Christian art, showing that what had not existed in the Empire before 313 came on the scene at the time of Constantine's death. Before moving on, however, we should note two caveats to these conclusions. The first is Thomas Matthews' argument that Christian art in the fourth century in no way reflects a Greco-Roman influence.[80] According to Matthews, it is a mistake to attribute a so-called "Emperor mystique" to Christian art. We need look no further than the New Testament to explain the ways in which early Christian artists depicted Christ, which both before and after Constantine register a rigorous protest against the Roman

---

77 Beskow, *Rex Gloriae*, 23.

78 Ibid., see n. 3.

79 MacCormack, *Art and Ceremony*, Pls. 33-4. MacCormack does not give the date for the plaque. In the context of MacCormack's plates, we infer that it dates to the fourth or fifth century; cf. a "city gate" sarcophagus showing, among other scenes, Elijah ascending to heaven and reaching for the descending hand of God, Gough, *Christian Art*, 110, Pl. 93 (date not given).

80 Thomas F. Matthews, *The Clash of Gods: A Reinterpretation of Early Christian Art* (Princeton: Princeton University Press, 1993).

pantheon and the deification of Caesar. The second caveat comes from André Grabar,[81] who concludes that Constantine's reforms barely affect Christian art, which does not begin to take on the characteristics familiar to us as "Byzantine" until the reign of Theodosius. That is, the traditional motifs in Christian art far outnumber the imperial, even after Constantine's death.

We can answer Matthews in part by rehashing the three cases above. Matthews' insistence that Christian art in no way resembles Greco-Roman art, therefore, shrinks in the face of the data at hand; he must account for what is there. His argument, however, is a useful corrective against MacCormack's equally unbalanced certitude, which we see when he describes the transformation of the depictions of Christ's triumphal entry:

> Somewhat later, the donkey gradually acquired the look of a horse and Christ, instead of holding a scroll, held the reins of his mount, his attitude and manner of entry becoming thereby more imperial....Christ's entry in Jerusalem is a New Testament theme, but the manner of communicating this theme became imperial in the fourth century, when it was depicted in visual art in the iconography of imperial arrivals.[82]

No doubt some Christian artists used their media to protest the idea of Rome's pantheon and Caesar's divinity, and not until much later did Christian artists regularly produce muscular and sensuous nudes like the Greeks and Romans had done. On the other hand, a "war of images"[83] was not

---

81 André Grabar, *Early Christian Art: From the Rise of Christianity to the Death of Theodosius*, Translated by Stuart Gilbert and James Emons (New York: Odyssey Press, 1968), 279.

82 MacCormack, *Art and Ceremony*, 65.

83 Matthews, *The Clash of Gods*, 4.

the universal aim of all early Christian artisans or of their sponsors, as the three cases treated above demonstrate.

Grabar's comments, therefore, present a subtler and more useful understanding of the data. Although it seems reasonable to conclude that Christian art begins to adopt some imperial themes in the fourth century, whether in acceptance or protest, Christianity by no means wholeheartedly takes over imperial imagery. Christian artisans faithfully continue to chisel biblical scenes from the Jonah cycle to the Good Shepherd to Christ before Pilate, and these tableaus make up the bulk of Christian art in that era.[84]

Accordingly, in this chapter we have examined two separate sets of data, both of which indicate that in the fourth century Christianity changed, and it reflected this change in three visible media. Up until 313 it had been profoundly ambivalent about—and at times openly hostile towards—"Pagan" religion in all forms, especially the cult of the Emperor, and now it found itself reciprocating the legitimacy that Constantine had granted it. This change comes through in the language of Christian writers, and in the transformation of Christian architecture and art. We may account for the flowering of Christian architecture—in contrast to the subtle changes in language and art—by pointing out that the magnificent basilicas in Rome and Palestine were the gifts of Constantine to the Church.[85] He dictated the terms of their splendor while the Church clung comfortably to its traditional expression in other media, introducing imperial motifs here and there in its art, and accommodating the panegyrists in its writings.

---

84 Grabar, *Early Christian Art*, 238-78.
85 Ibid., 279.

Using as a model the scholarship reviewed in this chapter, what implications may we now draw about the liturgy itself? This is the problem treated in the next chapter.

Chapter 4.
The Processional

Having seen how scholars understand the relationship between Church and state, as fourth century authors and artists worked it out, we now wish to discover if a similar link exists between the liturgy and state ceremony. Specifically, we want to know if the liturgy, like Christian art, began a slow transformation, gradually incorporating elements of civil and imperial ceremonies, or whether, along with Christian architecture, it quickly grew to grand proportions. One could predict that we will find elements of both forms of change. We may see that both Constantine's basilicas and the liturgy they housed were designed proportionate to one another, while the liturgy everywhere else remained more conservative, incorporating some aspects of state ceremony as Constantine's basilicas began to set the standards for worship in all parts of the Empire.

We have some evidence for supposing that whatever solemn ceremonies had embodied the liturgy before 313 were now embellished and enlarged in much the same way as the church buildings were themselves. In fact, I argue that the church buildings were adapted to accommodate the adapted liturgy. Specifically, I propose to show that whether or not a processional existed prior to the fourth century, it is reasonable to think that after 313 the liturgy began and ended with a grand processional that took on the solemnity and magnificence of imperial processionals and other state parades. The case rests on three pieces of evidence.

The *Adventus* of the Emperor

The ceremony of the *adventus* of the Emperor or other state officials, which appeared in the first century C.E. and continued through the time of the Tetrarchs and on into the Byzantine centuries, provides a possible model for the Christian processional. MacCormack describes this occasion in his *Art and Ceremony in Late Antiquity*: a typical *adventus* was a solemn affair in which the population of a city came forth from the walls to greet an arriving Caesar and conducted him back to the forum. The ceremony included singing hymns to Caesar, dancing, playing instruments, and sometimes the delivery of two speeches written by a panegyrist, one outside the walls and one inside the city.[86] Often the visit was an occasion for the Emperor to grant special favors to the city. This was sometimes depicted on coins or medallions minted to commemorate the event.[87]

One of the most famous *adventi* was Constantine's triumphal entry into Rome in 312, which is recorded on his arch (Fig. 21). The scenes show Constantine in a carriage, entering Rome accompanied by foot soldiers and cavalry. No citizens come forth to meet the Emperor, but side panels on the arch show Constantine enthroned and surrounded by subjects in the forum: in a top panel he addresses the crowd, in the bottom he distributes gifts (Fig. 22).[88]

Upon his arrival in the forum, the panegyrists spoke of Caesar as *deus praesens*,[89] the god who was available for aid and protection by his very presence. The language of the panegyrists reflected this apotheosis, as in this hymn reputedly sung to Demetrius Poliocretes as he entered Athens:

---

86 MacCormack, *Art and Ceremony*, 17-22.
87 Ibid., Pls. 9, 10.
88 Ibid., Pls. 12-5.
89 Ibid., 22-33.

> Other gods indeed are a great distance away
> Or have no ears,
> Or they do not exist or take no notice of us.
> But you we see present,
> Not made of wood or stone, but truly.[90]

MacCormack claims that the pattern of the *adventus* formed the template for "the different types of arrivals of Christ and of arrivals of bishops and of relics,"[91] and he appeals to Egeria's description of the reenactment of Palm Sunday in Jerusalem and Chrysostom's account of the translation of St. Thomas' relics to his martyrium near Constantinople.[92]

MacCormack's assertion is attractive because it appears to confirm our hypothesis, but he supplies no evidence to support his claim. Thus we must make up the deficit, and review the data that links *adventus* with the liturgical procession. In order to do this, first we turn to the eighth century stational mass.

The Stational Mass

As MacCormack describes it, the pattern of *adventus* finds a counterpart in Jungmann's description of Roman stational services in the seventh century,[93] which he derives from *Ordo Romanus I*.[94] Here the Bishop of Rome proceeds on horseback from the Lateran to the designated church. A "stately procession"[95] of the papal court accompanies him:

90 Athenaeus, VI, 253 in Ibid., 23.

91 Ibid., 64.

92 Ibid., 64-5.

93 Joseph A. Jungmann, *The Mass of The Roman Rite: Its Origins and Development*, 2 vols., trans. Francis A. Brunner (Benzinger Brothers, 1951 [Replica edition 1986 by Christian Classics]), I, 67-74.

94 *PL* 78, 937-948.

95 Jungmann, *Mass of the Roman Rite*, 67.

acolytes and legal administrators afoot, deacons and chief dignitaries of the Apostolic Palace mounted. Upon the Pope's arrival at the church, the gospel precedes him down the nave to the altar. This procession is observed by the bishops and presbyters of the titular churches, who are already seated on their benches lining the apse, and by the crowds who have arrived in procession from the seven regions of Rome. When the Pope has been properly attired in the *secretarium* near the entrance, he too proceeds to his throne at the vertex of the apse, accompanied by the tones of the introit. At the end of the service another procession returns the Pope to the *secretarium*.[96]

Jungmann makes several connections between this ceremony and "the ancient and originally oriental court ceremony"[97]: as the Pope processes to the altar, clerics bring incense, seven acolytes bear torches in his honor, and two deacons kiss his hands as they conduct him down the nave. Jungmann thinks all these rituals hearken back to honors due to the Emperor and other state officials.[98] For our part, we may make a connection between the processional as Jungmann describes it, and what we see on Constantine's arch. In both, a processional conducts the honoree in "gorgeous pomp"[99] to a throne where, surrounded by officials and crowds, he presides over a solemn ceremony. Neither processional is made up of civilians or laypeople, but rather of either clerics or soldiers, both on foot and in the saddle. The honoree himself is astride a horse, although in this case Constantine is in a carriage. Furthermore, three distinct symbols represent God's presence in the stational church, a counterpart to Caesar as *deus praesens* within the city:

---

96 Ibid., 67-73.
97 Ibid., 69.
98 Ibid., 68-9, n. 7.
99 Ibid., 73.

the Pope himself, the Gospel, and the elements of the Eucharist.[100]

I do not claim that a one-to-one correspondence links the two ceremonies, especially because the mass cannot compete with state parades in sheer size and grandeur, but the similarities do invite speculation. That is, we may hypothesize that when the Church designed its stational processions, its template was the state pomp with which it was already familiar. Where we have difficulty is in claiming that the stational mass begins as early as the fourth century, when the earliest descriptions of these services come to us from the eighth century. We may conjecture that these masses existed before they were codified in *Ordo Romanus I*, but the evidence does not allow us to claim that by the time any processional was officially recorded, it had already survived, in some form, for four hundred years.

Thus we return to Jungmann, who also describes three other processions that are part of the liturgy: the introit, the Little Entrance, and the Great Entrance. With these three Jungmann again appeals to court ceremony as models for what the Church did. There are two problems with Jungmann's reconstruction, however. First, the Little and Great Entrances, which bring in the Gospel and offerings respectively,[101] do not proceed down the nave of the basilica, but enter through a side door and march around the altar. Thus they do not fit into the picture of what I am trying to show, that the church basilica accommodates a processional down the nave. Second, Jungmann is answered by a counter argument, this one from Gregory Dix, who, like Deissmann, White, and Matthews, looks no further than the early Church—and to Judaism before that—for the origin of

---

100 Ibid., 446-7; MacCormack, *Art and Ceremony*, 18.

101 Jungmann, *Mass of the Roman Rite*, 263-4; Gregory Dix, *The Shape of the Liturgy* (London: Dacre Press, 1964 [reprint of 1945 ed.]), 120.

liturgical ceremony. He admits that the fourth century produced "a certain elaboration of ceremony" in the performance of the Eucharist, specifically in "the introit chant, which covered the processional entrance of the clergy."[102] He does not, however, think that this more elaborate ceremony incorporated any aspects of Greco-Roman cultus—not in the vestments, insignia, lights, or incense.[103]

The evidence does not necessarily lead to such a position, however. For one thing, it is possible that prior to 313 the Church liturgy included processions, but on a modest scale[104]: neither the congregation nor the churches were ample enough for a large and ostentatious parade. For another, whereas there is reason to doubt that the Church had grand parades prior to the fourth century, the state did have them. Thus, it is also reasonable to surmise that state pomp provided the template, at least for the stational procession.

We are still plagued, however, by the dates that we can assign to the origin of any processional. Jungmann admits that his description of the entrance or opening rite is a "construction,"[105] but he does not tell us how early he thinks it began. Dix also offers no evidence for placing the processional in the fourth century. Thus our next step is to turn away from the *Ordo Romanus I* and toward earlier works to search for the origins of the processional.

Processional in the Canonical Gospels

Before proceeding with the sources that describe early Christian liturgy, however, we ought to take a look at the

---

102 Dix, *The Shape of the Liturgy*, 397.

103 Ibid., 397-433.

104 I will argue this below in the discussion of Justin Martyr.

105 Jungmann, *Mass of the Roman Rite*, 267.

earliest Christian writings that describe anything that looks like a processional.

Paul's Epistle to the Colossians contains an ambiguous reference: "Wiping out the charge against us which was in decrees hostile to us, he has also removed it from us, having nailed it to the cross. He has divested himself of rule and authority and made a pubic example of them, triumphing over them by it."[106] Translators have chosen several ways to render θριαμβεύσας αὐτοὺς ἐν αὐτῷ. The NASB says, "having triumphed over them through Him." On the other hand, Zerwick and Grosvenor choose language that has implications for our hypothesis: according to them θριαμβεύσας...ἐν αὐτῷ means "lead around (as, e.g., prisoners) in a triumphal procession...by it (the cross)." This language brings to mind Caesar's triumphal processionals, and the image of the cross certainly recalls later liturgical processions.

Paul's language, however, gives us no evidence to claim that Paul links Christ's triumph to Christian worship in any way. We may speculate, however, that as early as Paul's writings Christians already pictured Christ as triumphant, and Paul expressed that idea in language that recalled the triumphs of Caesar.

We have already discussed a second example in the section on Christian art above. The canonical gospels all describe Jesus' so-called "triumphal entry" into Jerusalem, and John's gospel in particular provides a familiar image:

> The next day, when the great throngs that had come to the festival heard that Jesus was coming to Jerusalem, they took branches of palm trees and went out to meet him, shouting, "Hosanna! Blessed is he who comes in the name of the Lord, the King of Israel!" Finding a

106 Col. 2:14-15.

> young donkey, Jesus sat on it, just as it is written: "Fear not, daughter of Zion. Look, your king is coming, sitting on a donkey's colt."[107]

Here we see some elements that are familiar to us from the *adventus* and from the later stational mass: the citizens, hearing of Jesus' arrival, go out to meet him; they call him "King"; Jesus rides something like a horse; the people conduct him into the city. All of the elements are present in this celebration for us to liken it to an impromptu *adventus*.

The similarities between this New Testament event and state ceremony are difficult to ignore. In this case, it appears that the method of Jesus' final entry into Jerusalem is not an accident, but designed—whether by himself or John's redactor, I cannot say—to resemble an imperial *adventus*. Thus, apparently, either when first century Jews greeted Jesus outside of Jerusalem, or when the authors of the next generation recorded the event, they gave it the structure of grand pomp with which they were familiar. We may thus argue that the model of the *adventus* was in place in Christian Scriptures as early as John's Gospel, and perhaps earlier in the canonical Gospels. What we must do now is show that beyond depicting Christ in royal tableaus, the Church acted out the triumph of Christ with some sort of liturgical pageantry in the fourth century or earlier.

Processional in Justin Martyr

Because no formal liturgical order tells us of grand or solemn pomp in the fourth century mass, we turn now to other Christian authors of late antiquity to search for mentions of a "processional." In the Greek authors we

107 John 12:12-15.

search for the verb πομπεύω and its derivative noun πομπή; in the Latin, for *procedo* and its derivatives.[108]

One of the earliest possible mentions of the processional comes from the *First Apology* of Justin Martyr (d. 162-7 C.E.). While defending Christianity against the charge of atheism, Justin says,

> We have learned that this alone is worthy of Him: not to consume by fire those things He has brought into being for our sustenance, but to offer those things to ourselves and to the needy, and thus being thankful, to conduct processions and hymns through speech ....[109]

Lampe's rendering of πομπὰς as "solemnities" assumes that Justin refers to the entire Eucharistic service rather than its opening rite alone.[110] Leslie Barnard translates it the same way (πομπὰς...πέμπειν = "celebrating our solemnities"[111]), arguing that while the word usually means "a solemn procession," the text requires a less specific meaning, because a procession would bring undue attention and therefore persecution to any congregation in Justin's day.[112] Barnard's assertion, however, seems out of place, for

---

108 Other words in the same semantic field (ἀπάντησις, κωμάζω, and σεμνόω in Greek; *apparatus*, *commissatio*, *ostentatio*, and *triumphus* in Latin) do not appear to be technical liturgical terms in Christian authors.

109 μόνην ἀξίαν αὐτοῦ τιμὴν ταύτην παραλαβόντες, τὸ τὰ ὑπ᾽ ἐκείνου εἰς διατροφὴν γενόμενα, οὐ πυρὶ δαπανᾷν, ἀλλ᾽ ἑαυτοῖς καὶ τοῖς δεομένοις προσφέρειν, ἐκείνῳδὲ εὐχαρίστους ὄντας, διά λόγου πομπὰς καὶ ὕμνους πέμπειν...; Justin Martyr, *Apol. I*, 13 (*PG* 6, 315).

110 G.W.H. Lampe, *A Patristic Greek Lexicon* (Oxford: Clarendon Press, 1961), 1120.A.

111 *St. Justin Martyr,The First and Second Apologies*, trans. Leslie William Barnard (Mahwah, N.J.: Paulist Press, 1997), 30.

112 Ibid., 115-6, n. 75.

presumably second century Christians conducted their Eucharistic worship clandestinely, in the privacy of their house churches. On the other hand, in context πέμπειν makes sense as "to conduct," connoting "to convoy" or "to escort"[113] rather than its more common meaning "to send" or Barnard's "celebrating." Not only so, but Justin mentions hymns accompanying the πομπὰς, which sounds like what we know of the later introit, as described by Jungmann above. Justin's language suggests that the solemn rituals to which he refers include one or more processionals.

The use of πομπὴν πέμπειν to mean, "to conduct a processional" occurs in at least five ancient sources (Herodotus 5.56, Aristophanes *Ecclesiazusae* 757, Thucydides 6.56, Lysias 13.80, and Demosthenes 4.26[114]). But it is difficult to know how this information strengthens the argument, for these works all date from the fifth through the fourth centuries B.C.E. In light of the five to six centuries' gap between these authors and Justin, we can only suppose that this phrase and this usage would have been in his working vocabulary if he had been literate in the Greek classics.

Justin provides an example that suggests that solemn—if not grand—processions were a part of Christian worship early on. Because, however, processions are common in many different worship traditions, we need to link a grand and regal processional with Constantine's basilicas in the fourth century. For this we turn to the travel diary of Egeria.

---

113 *A Lexicon Abridged from Liddell and Scott's Greek-English Lexicon* (Oxford: Clarendon Press, 1963), 542.A.

114 H.G. Liddell and R. Scott, *A Greek-English Lexicon*, rev. with supplement, H.S. Jones, (Oxford: Clarendon Press, 1996), 1359.B.

Processional in Egeria

The pilgrim nun Egeria probably visited Palestine between 381 and 384,[115] spending much of her time worshiping in the many churches in and around Jerusalem. The liturgy that she describes burgeons with references to the motion of the congregation and bishop, both within and between churches. We will extract from Egeria's writings two types of information: first, we will search for outright mentions of processions; second, we will look for descriptions of various processions that she might not explicitly name *processiones*.

1. *Procedo* and its derivatives come up several times in Egeria's writing, most of them associated with two of Constantine's basilicas (the Holy Sepulcher and Eleona), and some with the church on Mt. Zion.[116] Michael Fraser is confident that when Egeria says *proceditur* she refers to the liturgical procession.[117] John Wilkinson, by contrast, never translates any instances of *procedo* as "the procession" or "they process," but always as "they assemble,"[118] although he does suppose that Egeria describes a processional[119] and translates one participle of *venio* as "their procession."[120] The text itself uses common verbs of motion, such as *ago*, *venio*, *ito*, *duco*, and *procedo* to describe worship that frequently moves worshipers and clergy from one church to another. When, on the other

115 John Wilkinson, *Egeria's Travels* (London: S.P.C.K., 1971), 3; 237-9.

116 Besides the attestations treated here, *procedo* appears in S. Siluiae, *Pereg.* 24.3, 27.3, 5, 6.

117 See Fraser's translation at, *Egeria and the Fourth Century Liturgy of Jerusalem* [hypertext version online] (University of Durham: Department of Theology, June 1994, accessed 30 July 1999); available from http://users.ox.ac.uk/~mikef/durham/egeria.html.

118 Wilkinson, *Egeria's Travels*, 89-147.

119 Ibid., 83.

120 Ibid., 130; S. Siluiae, *Pereg.* 27.8 (Geyer, 79).

hand, she means to say that the people "gather" or "assemble" for worship in this or that church, she uses *colligo*, apparently in contrast to these verbs of motion.[121] Context favors *procedo* to connote motion to or within a church, rather than gathering or assembling, as in the following example.

Describing regular Sunday worship, Egeria says,

> a. But at first light, because it is the Lord's day, they also process in the great church, which Constantine built on Golgotha behind the Cross, and there they do everything according to what is customary on the Lord's Day everywhere.[122]

If we maintain that *proceditur* connotes the movement of worshipers as a group rather than their gathering in one spot, then the use of *in* with the ablative rather than with the accusative (or *ad* with the accusative) implies that Egeria describes movement within the church itself rather than into or toward it. This language suggests a liturgical processional of some sort, as with several other examples:

> b. And throughout the year, every Lord's day, they process in the great church (the one on Golgotha behind the Cross), which Constantine built....[123]

> c. Then on the first [day of Easter], the day of the Lord itself, they process in the great church (that is to the Martyrium)—also on the second and third days.

---

121 See for example S. Siluiae, *Pereg.* 24.8, 43.3 (Geyer, 74, 94).

122 *Cum luce autem, quia dominica dies est, et proceditur in ecclesia maiore, quam fecit Constantinus, quae ecclesia in Golgotha est post Crucem, et fiunt omnia secundum consuetudinem, qua et ubique fit die dominica*; S. Siluiae, *Pereg.* 25.1 (Geyer, 74).

123 *Et cum toto anno semper dominica die in ecclesia maiore procedatur, id est quae in Golgotha est, id est post Crucem, quam fecit Constantinus....*; ibid., 25.6 (Geyer, 75).

> Accordingly, having made the mass, they always go with hymns from the Martyrium to the Anastasis. On the fourth day, however, they process in Eleona, on the fifth to the Anastasis, on the Sixth in Zion, on Saturday before the Cross; but on the Lord's day (that is on the eighth), once more in the great church (that is to the Martyrium).[124]

> d. From Easter to Pentecost] on Lord's Days, however, they always process in the Martyrium (the great church) in accordance with custom, and they go with hymns from there to the Anastasis. On the fourth day, however, and on the sixth day, since no one fasts on them, they process in Zion in the morning only; the mass is made in the usual order.[125]

> e. On these days of the dedications,[126] however, the adornment of all churches is exactly as it is at Easter or Epiphany, and through each successive day they process in different holy places in the same way as at Easter or Epiphany. For on the first and second day they process in the great church, which is called the Martyrium. Likewise on the third day [they process] in Eleona, in the church on the very mountain from which the Lord ascended after the passion, in which is

---

124 *Proceditur autem ipsa die dominica prima in ecclesia maiore, id est ad Martyrium, et secunda feria et tertia feria, ubi ita tamen, ut semper missa facta de Maryrio ad Anastase ueniatur cum ymnis. Quarta feria autem in Eleona proceditur, quinta feria ad Anastase, sexta feria in Syon, sabbato ante Cruce, dominica autem die, id est octauis, denua in ecclesia maiore, id est ad Martyrium*; ibid., 39.2 (Geyer, 91).

125 *Dominicus autem diebus semper in Martyrio, id est in ecclesia maiore, proceditur iuxta consuetudinem et inde itur ad Anastase cum ymnis. Quarta feria autem et sexta feria, quoniam ipsis diebus penitus nemo ieiunat, in Syon proceditur, sed mane; fit missa ordina suo*; ibid., 41 (Geyer, 93).

126 These are the "Encenia," the days commemorating the consecration of the Martyrium and Anastasis of the Holy Sepulcher, coinciding with the day on which the cross was discovered, as Egeria explains in the preceding paragraph.

> located the very cave where the Lord taught the apostles on the Mount of Olives. On the fourth day, however....[end of text][127]

Based on these examples, apparently Egeria describes two different sorts of processionals, one that takes place within a church, and one between churches: thus "they process...*to* the Anastasis" (proceditur...ad Anastase[128]) in example c. above. If this is the case, then the movement between churches appears to be an intrinsic part of worship.

Where can we find evidence that Egeria uses *procedo* in a technical sense? I have translated it as "they process," but Egeria may use it synonymously with other verbs of motion. What we need, therefore, is a context that shows us what Egeria means when she says *proceditur.* Besides these and other examples, Egeria uses a derivative of *procedo* twice more. One instance describes the rising of the sun:

> f. Then afterwards the mass is made from the Cross (before the sun rises), and straightway the energetic ones go on to Zion to pray at the column at which the Lord was flogged.[129]

---

127 *His ergo diebus enceniarum ipse ornatus omnium ecclesiarum est, qui et per pascha uel epiphania, et ita per singulos dies diuersis locis sanctis proceditur ut per pascha uel epiphania. Nam prima et secunda die in ecclesia maiore, quae appellatur Martyrium, proceditur. Item tertia die in Eleona, id est in ecclesia, quae est in ipso monte, a quo ascendit Dominus in caelis post passionem, intra qua ecclesia spelunca illa, in qua docebat Dominus apostolos in monte Olueti. Quarta autem die....*; S. Siluiae, *Pereg.*, 49.3 (Geyer, 101).

128 We do not know why Egeria uses *ad* with the ablative to connote motion towards. Wilkinson reports that J.H. Bernard, Egeria's original translator, complained about her grammar; *Egeria's Travels*, 5.

129 *Post hoc ergo missa facta de Cruce, id est antequam sol procedat, statim unusque animosi uadent in Syon orare ad columnam illam, ad quam flagellatus est Dominus*; ibid., 37.1 (Geyer, 83).

This example is significant because it suggests that Egeria uses *procedo* to connote motion rather than assembly, and in this case motion along a fixed and regular course—that is, a ritual activity. So we presume it is the same in the other cases as well.

It is the remaining instance of *procedo* that appears to provide the particular technical usage for which we search:

> g. Indeed, here the fortieth day of Epiphany is celebrated enthusiastically with highest distinction. For the same day the procession is in the Anastasis; everyone processes and everything goes in order with greatest rejoicing just as it does during Easter.[130]

Here *processio* is a nominative noun, serving as the subject of the sentence, and it appears to function technically to mean a liturgical procession. These two examples, therefore, suggest that Egeria consistently uses *procedo* to refer to ritual processionals that are regular parts of worship, both within the service, and when worshipers and clergy move from one church to another.

2. Having established that it is plausible to think that Egeria describes several processionals, we now turn to other instances when she does not, so far as we can tell, use technical language, but does appear to describe ritual processionals. Because the text contains numerous examples, two will suffice to demonstrate what I mean. Moving to Egeria's description of Lenten services we read:

> a. In Lent, as I said above, on the fourth day at nine, they process in Zion in accordance with what is customary the rest of the year....When, however, they

130 *Sane quadragesimae de epiphania ualde cum summo honore hic celebrantur. Nam eadem die processio est in Anastase et omnes procedunt et ordine suo aguntur omnia cum summa laetitia ac si per pascha*; ibid., 26.1 (Geyer, 77).

> have made the mass, the people lead the bishop with hymns from there all the way to the Anastasis; in this way they come so that when they enter the Anastasis it is in time for Lucernare.[131]

And describing the end of Lent Egeria says:

> b. So at the beginning of the seventh hour, everyone goes to the Lazarium, which is Bethany, perhaps in the second mile from the city. But on the way from Jerusalem into the Lazarium, perhaps fifty paces from the Lazarium, is a church on the pavement where Mary the sister of Lazarus met the Lord. When, therefore, the bishop has arrived, all the monks meet him and the people go in ....But when they have come to the Lazarium, such a great crowd has gathered that not only that place itself, but also all the fields around are full of people.[132]

Although Egeria does not label these movements of the bishop, the language strongly suggests that they are formal, ritual processionals. First, the events are at appointed times. Second, the people lead the bishop from one church to the other, much as the army conducted Caesar from one city to the other in an *adventus* (and the people led him from the city gates into the forum), and as the clergy escorted the Pope

---

131 *Diebus uero quadragesimarum, ut superius dixi, quarta feria ad nona in Syon proceditur iuxta consuetudinem totius anni....Cum autem facta fuerit missa, inde cum ymnis populus deducet episcopum usque ad Anastasem; inde sic uenitur, ut cum intratur in Anastase, iam et hora lucernari sit*; ibid., 27.6 (Geyer, 79).

132 *Ac sic ergo cum coeperit se hora septima facere, omnes ad Lazarium ueniunt. Lazarium autem, id est Bethania, est forsitan secundo miliario a ciuitate. Euntibus autem de Ierusolima in Lazarium forsitan ad quingentos passus de eodem loco ecclesia est in strata in eo loco, in quo occurrit Domino Maria soror Lazari. Ibi ergo cum uenerit episcopus, occurrent illi omnes monachi, et populus ibi ingreditur....In Lazario autem cum uentum fuerit, ita se omnis multitudo colligit, ut non solum ipse locus, sed et campi omnes in giro pleni sint hominibus*; ibid., 29.4-5 (Geyer, 82).

from the Lateran to the appointed church in the later stational mass. Third, in example b. the bishop is met by waiting people twice, once by the clergy at the church by the road, and again by the assembled congregation at the Lazarium. This recalls both the populace gathering to receive Caesar, and the seven collected congregations assembled and awaiting the arrival of the Pope at the stational church. In another example from Egeria not treated here, the people arrive first at the Anastasis and then send for the bishop, who comes to find the congregation in place and ready for his service.[133]

Again, we cannot go so far as to claim a one-to-one correspondence between *adventus*, the stational mass, and Egeria's processions, but the similarities invite speculation. In all three, both conducting the official from place to place and his arrival at an appointed place and time are important rituals. Likewise, in Egeria these rituals resemble formal processions that are well established by the late fourth century. So all three examples of ritual movement share enough in common to allow us to make a plausible connection between them—to suppose that Egeria describes several processionals that resemble the *adventus*. Not only so, but in Egeria's diary, these processionals seem to be the shank of worship, connecting the other elements, seamlessly joining mass in one place to mass in another. Thus motion defines the worship that Egeria describes—movement from one place to the next—and verbs of motion make up the bulk of the action.

It is therefore striking to note that Egeria speaks of the Eucharist only once, on Thursday of Holy Week,[134] unless she means to include it in her phrase "they do everything

---

133 Ibid., 24.3 (Geyer, 71-2).

134 Ibid., 35.2 (Geyer, 85).

according to what is customary everywhere."[135] As a result, Egeria's language paints a word picture of a liturgy in motion—processionals leading the bishop from church to church and conducting him from the entrances and down the naves of various sanctuaries—punctuated by prayers, hymns, antiphons, readings, blessings, and an occasional offering.

In this chapter we have been able to show that very soon after their construction, the liturgy in Constantine's Palestinian churches included solemn, ritualistic movement. Based on Egeria's description, apparently this movement was in the form of processionals, both within the basilicas and from one basilica to another. These processions resemble both the grand processionals that were long a part of state ceremony, and those that the *Ordo Romanus I* codified in the eighth century. The evidence suggests that the Christian basilicas and the grand processionals emerge more or less simultaneously, that these churches (as well as Constantine's other churches) are designed as grand processional halls. I aim to strengthen this hypothesis in the following chapter by examining what I call a "control group" of basilical buildings.

---

135 Above, example a.

Chapter 5.
Basilical Synagogues

The preceding chapters have constructed the hypothesis that Constantine designed his basilical churches to accommodate a grand processional, and he did so by copying the design of a major colonnaded thoroughfare, such as the *cardo maximus.* The final step is to test the hypothesis by using a control group. Consequently, in this chapter we will investigate whether other religious structures display the same standardized features that Constantine's basilicas do.

Galilean synagogue basilicas provide an excellent test case for this task. Not only do these structures come on the scene roughly contemporary with the earliest church basilicas (the examples we will examine all come from the third through fifth centuries), but synagogue builders in the Galilee also almost uniformly constructed basilicas. What we wish to know is, did synagogue worship in these centuries include a grand processional, beginning at the entrance and proceeding down the axis of the nave? If it did, then we should expect to see a standardized design that accommodates this ritual, just as in Constantine's basilicas. If, on the other hand, synagogue worship had no processional comparable to that of Christian worship, then the opposite should be true: we not only should fail to find this design, but we should see another design that reflects the particular ethos of synagogue worship. By this I mean, as we have seen in Chapter 2, the character of synagogue worship should shape the worship space in some way.

Jewish Liturgy in the Formative Age

As with its Christian counterpart, the shape and content of Jewish liturgy in its formative age is largely conjecture, based on rabbinic sources that may not have defined a widely-practiced norm until much later than the time of their writing. Additionally, the *Seder Rav Amram*, which represents the earliest "fixed" liturgy, dates to the middle of the ninth century. It is here that the *Shema' Yisra'el* and *Tefillah* become central to worship in most services in Europe and the Middle East, according to Lawrence Hoffman.[136] The *Seder Rav Amram*, however, presents the same difficulty as the *Ordo Romanus* of the Christian liturgy: we may surmise that the elements of Jewish worship codified in the *Seder* had existed for some time before they were written down, but we do not know for how long.

As with the Christian liturgy and other writings, the Jewish liturgy of Late Antiquity used titles that the Greco-Roman world had reserved for Caesar. Hoffman says that the unique Rabbinic prose prayer known as the *berakhah* was in place by the third century. In the opening words of these benedictions, *baruch atah adonai melech ha'olam* ("Blessed art Thou, O Lord our God, King of the World"), one recognizes the titles—again finding their origin in the Jewish Scriptures—that the Empire used for Caesar and the Church for Christ: Lord, God, and King. They appear here as well, and they lead us to ask whether Judaism, like Christianity, was in some tension with the state. The answer must undoubtedly be yes. A second question, however, is Did the synagogue in Palestine, whose language about God paralleled the state's language about Caesar, ever appropriate state pomp in its worship, imperial images in its art, or regal

---

136 Lawrence Hoffman, "Jewish Liturgy and Jewish Scholaship," in *Judaism in Late Antiquity*, Part I, *The Literary and Achaeological Sources*, ed. Jacob Neusner (Leiden: E.J. Brill, 1995), 249-50.

proportions in its architecture? We find our answer in three examples from Jewish worship and art.

1. Two passages in the Mishnah appear to describe ritual processions, one associated with the festival of Sukkot, and another having to do with daily sacrifices in the temple. Neither procession, however, is analogous to the entrance processional of the Christian mass. The passage from M. Sukkah 4.5 reads as follows:

> A. The religious rite of the willow branch, how does it proceed?
> B. There was a place below Jerusalem called Mozah. They go down there and pick young willow branches, they bring them and set them up by the sides of the altar, and they bow their heads over the top of the altar.
> C. They sounded a plain note on the shofar, a quavering note, and a plain note.
> D. Every day they walk around the altar one time, and they say, "O Lord, save us we pray! O Lord, bring prosperity we pray (Ps. 118: 25)!"
> E. Rabbi Judah says, "[They say] '*'Ani waho*, save us we pray! *'Ani waho*, save us we pray!'
> F. On that day they walk around the altar seven times."
> G. What do they say when they leave the altar?
> H. "Praise to you, O altar! Praise to you, O altar!"
> I. Rabbi Eliezar says, "For the Lord and for you, O altar! For the Lord and for you, O altar!" [137]

Two difficulties with this passage tell us that this processional finds no match in Christian worship. First, none of its elements recall the *adventus* of the Emperor or the

137 My translation of this and the following passage follows the form critical divisions of Jacob Neusner's *The Mishnah: A New Translation* (New Haven and London: Yale University Press, 1988).

Christian rite: no honoree is paraded into the temple; rather, the honoree is the altar, which must remain stationary, and the processional moves around it. Second, we cannot show that this temple processional was a part of synagogue worship in the first through fourth centuries.

A second passage, Mishnah tractate Tamid 3.1, describes another temple processional:

> A. The superintendent said to them, "Come and draw lots [to decide] (1) who will slaughter [the victim], (2) who will sprinkle the blood, (3) who will remove the ashes of the inner altar, (4) who will remove the ashes of the lamp, (5) who will take up the limbs to the ramp:
> B. "(1) the head and the [right] hind leg, (2) and the two forelegs, (3) the rump and the [left] hind leg, (4) the breast and the neck, (5) and the two flanks, (6) the intestines, (7) and the fine flour, (8) and the cakes, (9) and the wine."
> C. They drew lots.
> D. Whoever won won.[138]

This processional appears to be the counterpart to the one that brought in the host in the Christian liturgy. The same problems apply here, however, as did with the earlier passage. Namely, on what basis may we suppose that this temple ritual was copied in the synagogue liturgy, which brought in no sacrifice? Furthermore, unlike the Christian processional, this processional could not have taken place through the midst of the congregation, for the pieces of the sacrificial victim might have contracted uncleanliness.

2. In later times a solemn processional does appear in Jewish worship, associated with the *simhat torah* ("Joy of the Torah"), the last day of Sukkot. Here, however, the Torah scrolls were paraded around the bema, rather than in the

---

138 Cf. Yoma 2.

entrance and down the axis of the nave.[139] This parade resembles the Great and Little Entrances in the Church liturgy more than the entrance processional of the bishop. Furthermore, although we can locate special readings assigned to this day in the Babylonian Talmud (Meg. 31a), we have no early references to the processional itself. Evidently we cannot place this ceremony any earlier than the Middle Ages, and we must possibly push it later than that.[140]

Thus we find nothing in the texts of Judaism's formative age that resembles state parades. What then of Jewish art?

3. Symbols in Jewish art form a more complicated category than Jewish ceremony, for here synagogues clearly borrowed Greco-Roman themes. The prime example of this is the pattern found on numerous mosaic synagogue floors in Palestine: the wheel of the zodiac with Helios at its center and the four seasons in their respective quarters. In the face of this commonplace and clearly "Pagan" imagery, we make two observations.

First, we know of no link between the zodiac and state religion that could lead us to hypothesize that a processional, or other ceremony resembling state parades, happened in these synagogues.[141] Rather, Goodenough finds

---

139 *Encyclopaedia Judaica*, s.v. "SIMHAT TORAH"; cf. Ismar Elbogen, *Jewish Liturgy: A Comprehensive History*, trans. Raymond P. Scheindlin (Philadelphia: The Jewish Publication Society, New York: The Jewish Theological Seminary of America, 1993 [German, 1913; Hebrew, 1972]), 160.

140 In rather confusing language Elbogen says, "by the end of the Middle Ages we find [these processions] in every country," ibid., but he then admits, "no Medieval source mentions the processions on the Joy of the Torah," ibid., 429, n. 8.

141 Erwin R. Goodenough, *Jewish Symbols in the Greco-Roman Period* (New York: Pantheon Books, 1953-1965), Vol 1, 178-267; Vols 7-8; Vol.

in these images elements of a mystical Judaism not represented in the rabbinic documents. In Goodenough's language, the zodiac and other "Pagan" symbols comprise a "symbolic vocabulary."[142] In Jacob Neusner's language they are a "symbolic discourse in iconic form."[143] The discourse, of which these symbols form meaningful statements, so far as we can tell, has nothing to do with grand ceremony, but instead reflects the ethos of a mysticism.

Second, the most common images found in synagogues[144]—the ethrog, lulav, shofar, and menorah—have no discernible connection to Greco-Roman iconography. That is, they are peculiar to Jewish art; we may link them with the major festivals of Sukkot, Rosh Hashanah/Yom Kippur, and Hanukkah respectively,[145] but so far as we know, they have no connection with solemn processionals.

Thus, three examples from Jewish liturgy and art demonstrate that the Judaisms of the formative age have no interest in recapitulating or appropriating the elements of Roman worship and ceremony. The Mishnah and other texts mention no processionals (or any other rituals that might lead us to infer the presence of processionals), and the Jewish art from the period of the Talmuds suggests the same conclusion. The question before us now is, If the liturgy of formative Judaism had no grand processional, do Galilean basilical synagogues look like Christian basilicas?

12, 132-57; and Jacob Neusner, *Symbol and Theology in Early Judaism* (Minneapolis: Fortress Press, 1991).

142 Goodenough, *Jewish Symbols*, Vol. 12, 42.

143 Neusner, *Symbol and Theology*, 142-75.

144 So common that Neusner says "they occur with disproportionate frequency" in comparison with the some 100 other images found in synagogues; ibid., 171.

145 Ibid., 187-8.

Galilean Synagogues

Strange notes that some twenty synagogues in the Galilee share "one architectural feature that seems to be almost a constant; it is the habit of their builders to place a row of columns between the benches against the walls and the central worship space."[146] That is, like the Christian basilica, Galilean synagogues share a standardized design. Strange goes on to observe, "This is a most peculiar arrangement, given the habit of the Romans to place rows of columns behind the backs of gathered spectators...."[147] This interior columniation creates a basilica that in many ways is indistinguishable from the many church basilicas that spring up in Palestine from the fourth through the seventh centuries. If this is so, how does one tell a Galilean synagogue from a church?

The chief method for archaeologists to distinguish a synagogue from an early Byzantine church is naturally through the decoration of the walls and floors, and through inscriptions. But how might archaeologists conducting a surface survey tell these structures apart were they to encounter the foundations of one on the ground and in surrounding vegetation, where decorations and inscriptions were invisible? If we were to encounter buildings of roughly the same size and surface pottery dating to the fourth or fifth century, at a site known to have housed both Jewish and Christian populations, what might distinguish the synagogue from the church? The simplest answer would be to count the rows of columns and to locate the entrances. As we have noted, we could be nearly certain that the church would have

---

146 James F. Strange, "First Century Galilee from Archaeology and from the Texts," in Douglas Edwards and Thomas McCollough, eds., *Archaeology and the Galilee: Texts and Contexts in the Graeco-Roman and Byzantine Periods* (Atlanta: Scholars Press, 1997), 43-4.

147 Ibid., 43.

only two rows of columns running the length of the building, east to west, and the main entrance would pierce the short western wall opposite the apse in the east. We could be almost equally certain that the synagogue would have three rows of columns arranged in a "horseshoe" around the nave. We might even call the presence of "heart-shaped" columns[148] an indicator of a synagogue versus a church.

In order to establish the regularity of these features, which we may also call a standardized design, I present three well-known Galilean synagogues as representatives of the genre.

1. The Meiron Synagogue (interior 28.4 m x 13.6 m; Fig. 23) was built in the late third century[149] in one of the four major villages of the Upper Galilee, of which Khirbet Shema' is another.[150] A tri-portal entrance in the short south wall, which was still standing up to two of the lintels when the team began excavating in 1971,[151] offers access into the nave and two side aisles from a colonnaded porch, while a hypothetical small entrance pierces the east wall near the southeast corner. Thus, like church basilicas, the building is oriented along the long axis. Unlike a church basilica, however, the building runs north-south, with a row of four columns across the back (i.e. north) wall. The two outer columns of this row are heart-shaped, forming corners with the side colonnades. Unlike those in a Christian basilica, the

148 "Heart-shaped" columns stand at the corners of rows, and when viewed in cross section from above, they have one "lobe" in line with one row, and another at right angles in line with the other row; see Figs. 24 and 26.

149 The excavation's Stratum IV; Eric M. Meyers, James F. Strange, and Carol L. Meyers, *Excavations at Ancient Meiron* (Cambridge, MA: The American Schools of Oriental Research, 1981), xviii, 16.

150 Ibid., 3.

151 The eastern portal was reconstructed in 1950; ibid., 9.

columns form a horseshoe shape, with the open end facing south toward the entrance.

2. The synagogue at Kh. Shema' (interior apr. 12 m x 9.26 m[152]; Fig. 24) was first constructed in the mid to late third century[153] and reconstructed in the fourth.[154] The later synagogue was built upon the foundations of, and to the dimensions of, the earlier synagogue. Both structures were oriented east-west and had two entrances: one in the long north wall offset west of center (letting into the north aisle between columns 1 and 2 of the north row), and another stepping down into the south aisle from an adjoining room to the west. Thus, although both buildings had only two rows of columns running longitudinally along the axis (no heart-shaped columns mark the corners[155]), there is nothing to indicate that these buildings focus traffic down the length of the nave.[156] On the contrary, both synagogues had benches along the north and west walls, with a corner bench in the southeast. The earlier synagogue had a bench on the south wall as well, which the second synagogue mostly covered with a bema.[157] Apparently, therefore, the architecture focused attention into the center of the room and toward the long south wall closest to Jerusalem.

---

152 These are my calculations from the stone-by stone ground plan in Eric M. Meyers, A. Thomas Kraabel, and James F. Strange, *Ancient Synagogue Excavations at Khirbet Shema'* (Durham, NC: Duke University Press, 1976), 40, Figure 3.4.

153 The excavation's Stratum III; ibid., 31, 45-64.

154 Stratum IV; ibid., 31, 64-81.

155 Ibid., 61-63.

156 See especially the isometric drawing of the synagogue with traffic patterns; ibid., 59, Fig. 3.10.

157 Ibid., 54-5, 68-9, 71-3.

3. The date of the synagogue at Capernaum (interior 23.1 x 17.26 m[158]; Fig. 25) is disputed, although the evidence for a late fourth or early fifth century date seems irrefutable based on the pottery and thousands of coins found in two hoards beneath the floor.[159] Capernaum's synagogue floor plan looks much like Meiron's: three rows of interior columns form a horseshoe that is open on the south, and heart-shaped columns mark the northwest and northeast corners. In addition, the tri-portal entrance in the south wall opens into the nave and side aisles, while a smaller entrance in the long east wall offers access to a colonnaded porch on that side, and another in the northwest corner leads to a small room. Two-tiered benches run the length of the east and west walls. Again, these features indicate that the building is not designed to accommodate or encourage two-way traffic flow, but focuses worshippers' attention toward the center of the nave.

What can we conclude about the design of Galilean synagogues in late antiquity? We know that their standardized design makes no accommodation for a processional down the nave, but why, then, is the design standardized at all? Strange finds a simple explanation by appealing to Herod's Temple, and to the ethos of recreating its sacred space.[160] Just as in the temple one watched the

---

158 These are my measurements of the plan—west wall north to south, and south wall east to west—in Virgilio C. Corbo, *Cafarnao.* Vol. I: Gli Edifici Della Citta (Jerusalem: Franciscan Printing Press, 1975), 116.

159 S. Loffreda, "The Late Chronology of the Synagogue of Capernaum," in Lee I. Levine ed., *Ancient Synagogues Revealed* (Jerusalem: Israel Exploration Society, 1981), 55-6.

160 J. F. Strange, "First Century Galilee," 43; cf. J. F. Strange, "Ancient Texts, Archaeology as Text, and the Problem of the First-Century Synagogue," in Howard Clark Kee and Lynn H. Cohick, eds. *Evolution of the Synagogue: Problems and Progress* (Harrisburg, PA: Trinity Press International, 1999), 27-45. Strange lays out this argument more completely in "The Synagogue as Metaphor," forthcoming in *Where We*

proceedings in the Court of Priests from the shade of the surrounding porticoes,[161] looking through columns in order to do so, so too in the Galilean synagogue one peers through columns into the central worship space.

Thus Strange presents a hypothesis that accounts for an architectural design, which in so many words he says is "standardized" ("one architectural feature that seems to be almost a constant," cited above). The Galilean synagogue recreates the sacred space of the Jerusalem temple. Strange points out that this ethos also explains the absence of interior columniation in several Samaritan synagogues excavated in the environs of Mt. Gerizim: Samaritans do not wish to recapitulate the design of the Jerusalem temple.[162] Strange's hypothesis, therefore, accounts both for his data and for its absence; one idea—the ethos of recreating the sacred space of the temple—explains both why Galilean synagogues place columns between the observer and the central worship space, and why Samaritan synagogues do not do so.

We now can explain both the standardized design of Constantine's basilicas, and the absence of that design in Jewish basilicas in the Galilee. We can also explain the standardized design of those synagogues, and the absence of that design in Samaritan synagogues. Constantine's basilicas replicate the feel of a broad avenue that bears a triumphal procession, while Galilean Jewish basilicas recreate the sacred space of the Second Temple. Why so? Because Galilean Jews have no interest in appropriating aspects of imperial pomp, their religious basilicas do not share the design of

---

Stand, vol. III, ed. Bruce D. Chilton, Alan J. Avery Peck, and Jacob Neusner (Leiden: Brill).

161 See Strange's reconstruction of the Second Temple plan in ibid., 45, Figure 2.

162 Ibid., 44.

Constantine's basilicas, but have their own design, inspired by an entirely different ethos.

Chapter 6.
Conclusion

Four questions regarding the development of the Christian basilica remain to be answered.

First, the hypothesis presented here does not explain the doubled aisles in four of Constantine's basilicas: the Lateran, St. Peter's, Holy Sepulcher, and Holy Nativity. One way to account for this feature is by appealing to the idea of grandiosity: doubling the aisles may simply make these churches all the more grand and monumental, befitting the commission of an Emperor.[163] In this case the high central nave flanked by columns still recapitulates the sense of a broad avenue.

Second, how do we know that the standardized design of Christian basilicas begins with Constantine's churches? Perhaps, by the time Constantine began constructing his churches, he simply took over a "design trend" that was already prevalent in the Empire. For example, the massive late third or early fourth century civil Basilica of Maxentius (interior dimensions of 82.40 x 62.70 m)—also called the Basilica of Constantine and Basilica Nova—is designed much like Constantine's church basilicas. It is laid out on a longitudinal axis, with only two side aisles running the length of the building, and with the tribunal apse in a short wall opposite a tri-portal entrance. It has some features, however, found in none of Constantine's other basilicas: four enormous piers partition the interior rather

---

163 Doubling of colonnades is common in all types of basilicas, as in the Basilica Ulpia (Fig. 8), and in the famous reference from Tosefta Sukka 1:5 to the double colonnade of the Alexandrian basilica-synagogue.

than colonnades, and cross vaults span the 25.30 meter-wide nave rather than roof timbers.[164] On the other hand, none of the basilicas that Constantine commissioned himself bear these rather significant architectural features. Consequently, building's design apparently reflects a passing aesthetic for civil basilicas rather than an enduring ethos. For example, the design is not repeated in the civil basilica at Sepphoris, treated in Chapter 2.

Third, some find the origin of Constantine's basilicas in the design of the Domus Flavia basilical hall.[165] In this elongated room a main entrance pierces a short wall opposite an apse in the other. Colonnades flank the nave, but stand too close to the walls to form true aisles. Also, as MacDonald points out, the interior colonnades are "dubious modern restorations,"[166] and the one restored column is out of place and disproportionate to the rest of the structure.[167] The layout of this room is thus too conjectural for us to hypothesize that it provided a template for the Constantinian basilica.

Finally, we have explored the Christian basilica as a solid metaphor for a Roman thoroughfare, and by this we have accounted for what we have called the Christian basilica's standardized design. It is possible, however, that more than one metaphor is in play here. For example, it is clear in Egeria that what we have called a "processional"—the ritual movement from church to church—may itself be a metaphor for pilgrimage. It is arresting to note that two of Constantine's basilicas in Palestine incorporate into their

---

164 G.T. Rivoira, *Roman Architecture and Its Principles of Construction Under the Empire* (New York: Hacker Art Books, 1972), 212-4.

165 MacDonald, *The Architecture of the Roman Empire*, I.53; see plan in Fig 6, B, p. 58 and Plates 40, 44.

166 Ibid., 53.

167 Ibid., Plate 39.

designs centralized church plans that become prominent in later memorial churches that define pilgrim routes. The Anastasis of the Church of the Holy Sepulcher surrounds the cave of the sepulcher with a circle of columns, and encloses these columns in a semi-circular structure (Fig. 4). Likewise, the Church of the Holy Nativity encloses the cave of the nativity in an octagon. The transept of St. Peter's in Rome, which houses the shrine to the saint, may be an example of cruciform architecture. These centralized plans are typical of memorial churches built in the fifth century, such as the octagonal churches over Peter's house in Capernaum and the church atop Mt. Gerizim. The Churches of the Sepulcher, Nativity, and St. Peter's are certainly over pilgrimage sites. It thus seems possible that if pilgrimage is a metaphor at play in the design of early Christian basilicas, then that metaphor continues in the later centralized churches that mark pilgrimage sites in Palestine and the rest of the Empire.[168]

Despite these unresolved issues, the hypothesis presented here proves to be reasonable by four criteria. 1) As demonstrated in Chapter 2, the plan of the aisles and naves of Constantine's basilicas mimics the layout of a colonnaded Roman thoroughfare. 2) In Chapter 3 we learned that church architecture appears to be one of several media in which fourth century Christians worked out the new relationship between Church and state, the other two being literature and art. Apparently, in the fourth century the Church openly expressed the idea of the kingship of Christ, long a part of their theology, now without fear of reprisal. 3) Chapter 4 showed that the adaptation of the liturgy from a private rite to a public ceremony works out the same idea in a fourth medium: worship. If Christ is King, we surmise that he is

---

168 See the discussion in Simon Coleman and John Elsner, "The Pilgrim's Progress: Art, Architecture, and Ritual Movement at Sinai," *World Archaeology* 26 No. 1 (June 1994): 73-89.

worthy of grand processionals celebrating his arrival and his enduring presence among his people. 4) Finally, Chapter 5 demonstrated that the hypothesis presented here explains both a phenomenon, when it occurs, and its absence, when it does not occur. By asking if the Constantinian basilica were modeled, at least in part, after the Roman thoroughfare, we were able to account, both for the standardized design of Constantine's basilicas, and for the absence of that design in synagogue basilicas. We said that A accounts both for B and for not-B, and by that token we have a plausible explanation for the design of Christian basilicas, a design that persists even up to the present.

This hypothesis should be sustained or revised as more data arises. Specifically, any theory of the origins of the Christian basilica will benefit from the unearthing of new inscriptions, texts, or Constantine's yet undiscovered basilicas.

Appendix 1: Figures

Figure 1. Isometric reconstruction of early 4th century church under San Crisogono, Rome. After a drawing by Frankl.

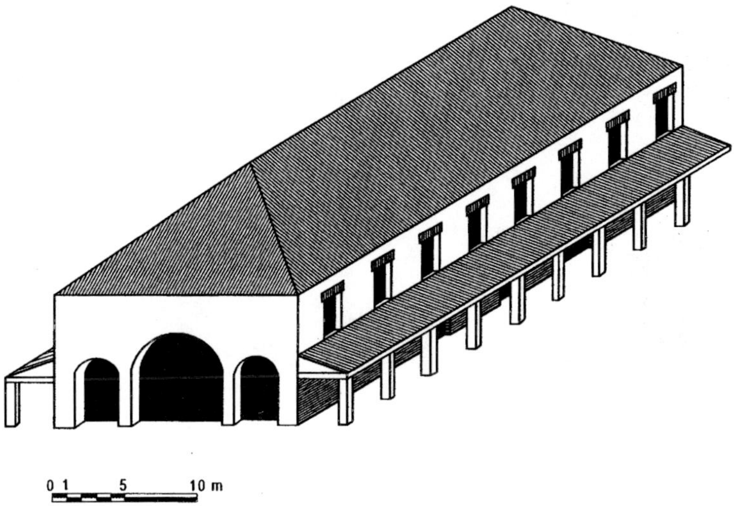

Figure 2. Old St. Peter's, Rome, based on the work of Tibero Alfarano.

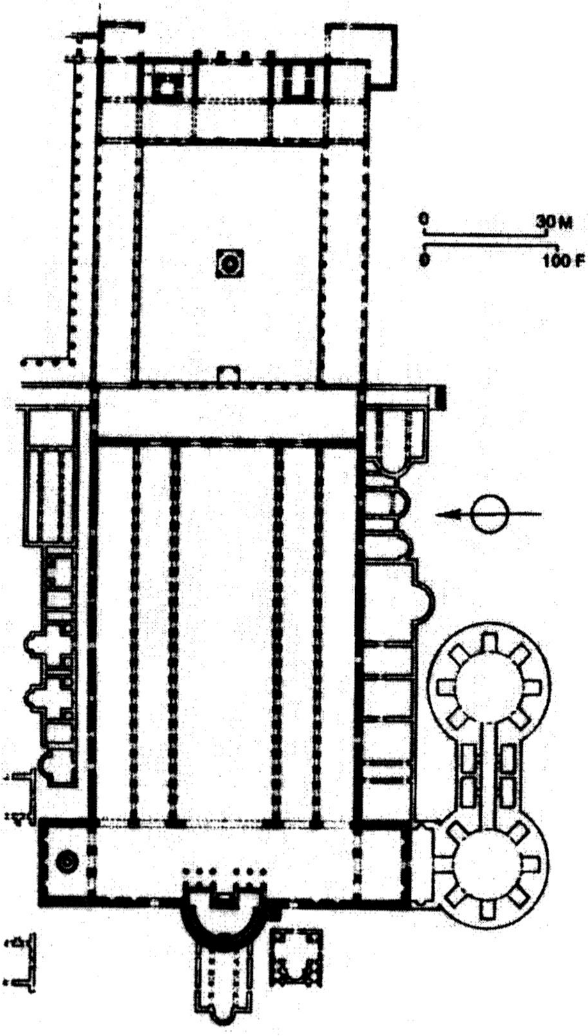

Figure 3. Excavations at Constantine's Church of St. John the Lateran, Rome. After a drawing by Corbett.

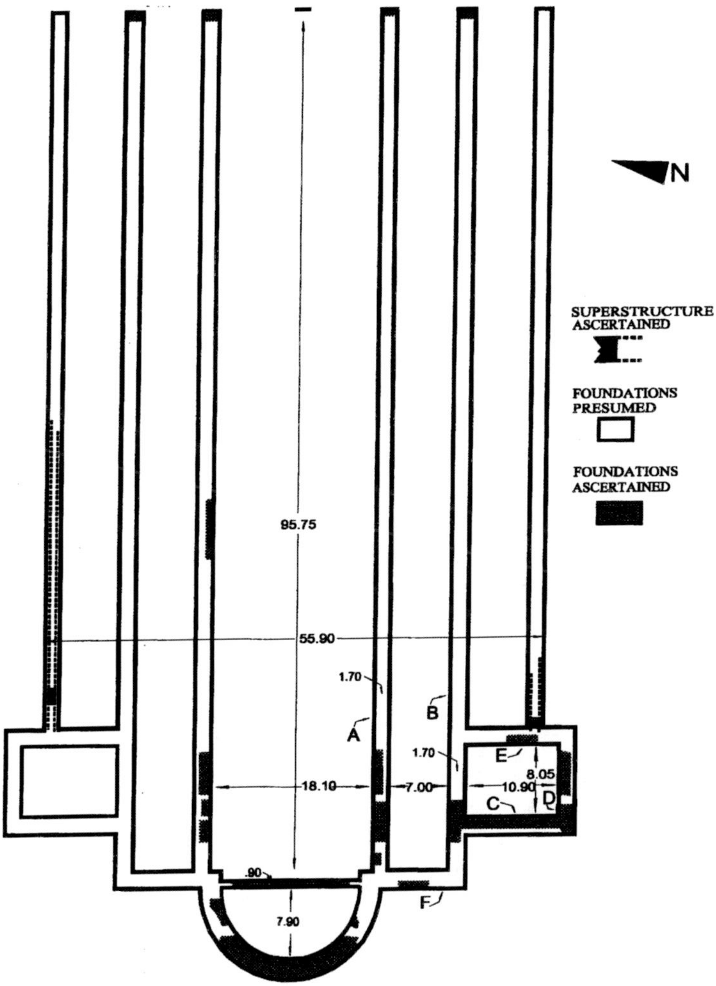

Figure 4. Constantine's Church of the Holy Sepulcher, Jerusalem. Drawing by Corbo.

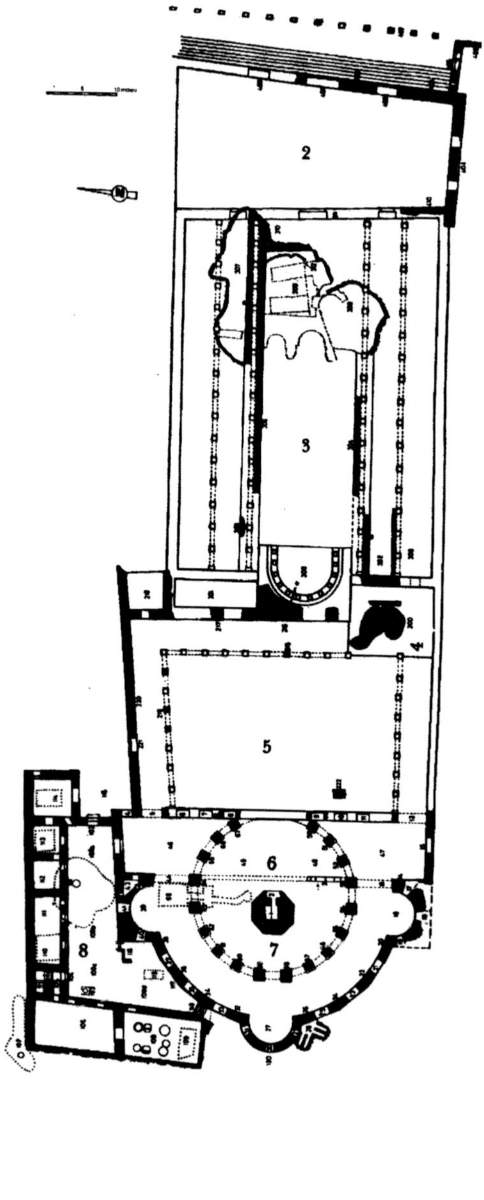

Figure 5. Constantine's Church of the Holy Nativity, Bethlehem. Drawing by Richmond.

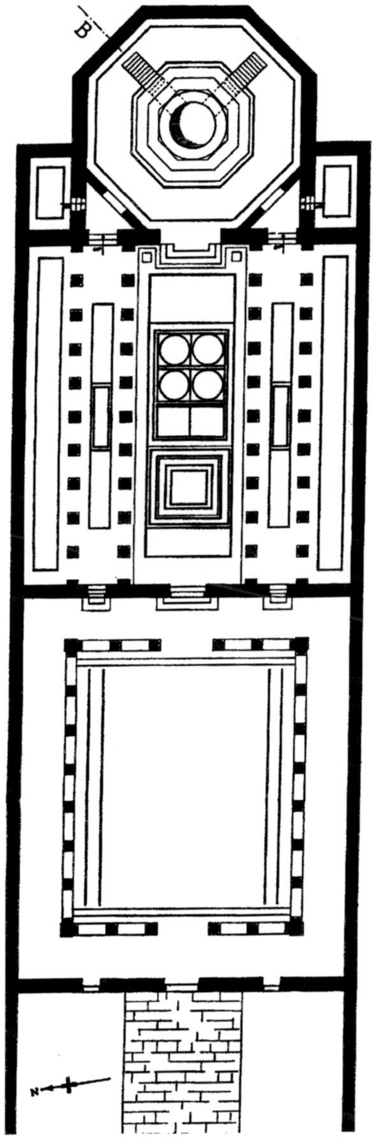

Figure 6. Constantine's Eleona church, Mt. of Olives. Drawing by Vincent.

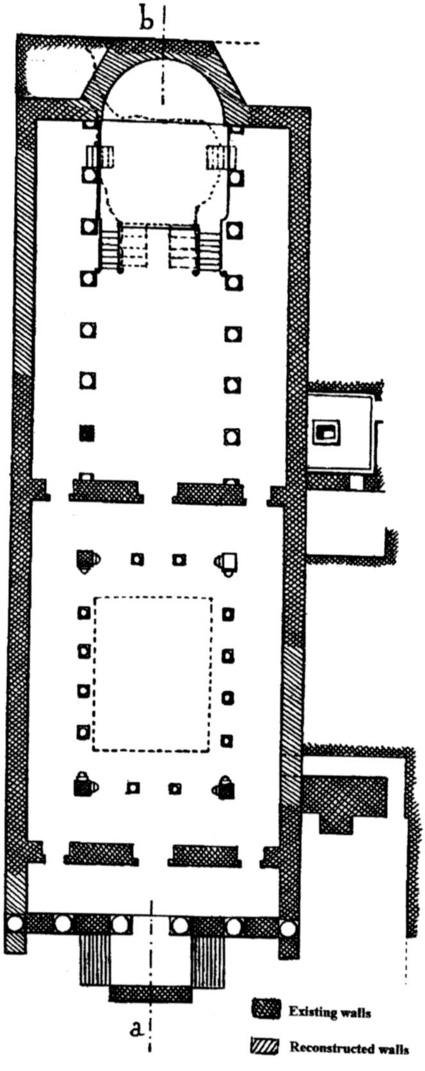

Figure 7. Fresco of the interior of the Lateran Basilica before 17th century.

Figure 8. Basilica Ulpia, Rome. Drawing by Macdonald.

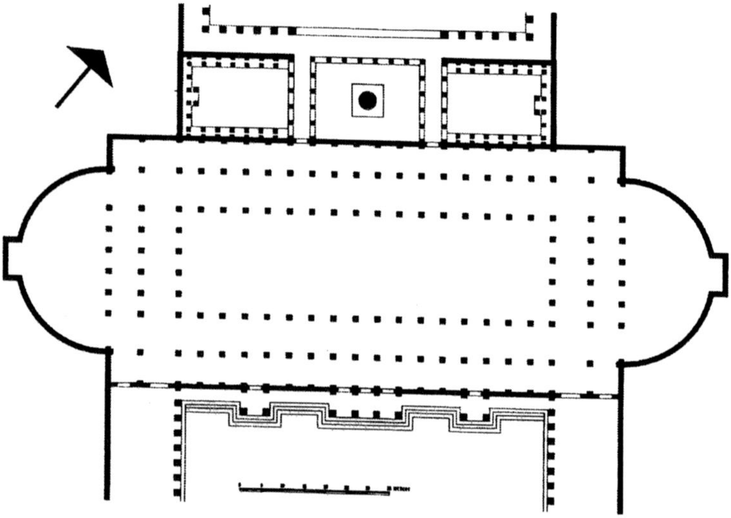

Figure 9. Basilica at Pompeii. After a drawing by Durum.

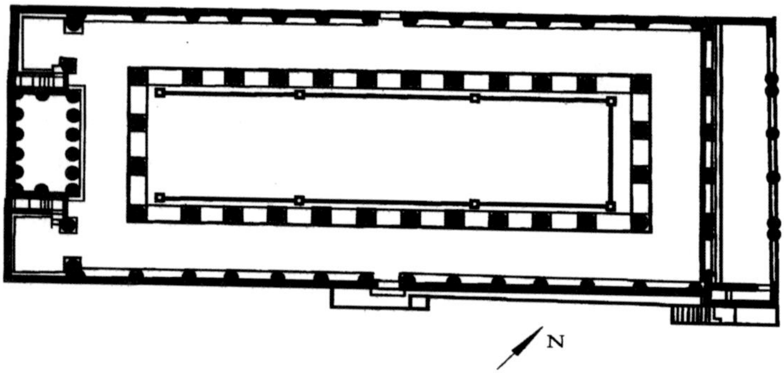

Figure 10. Vitruvius' basilica at Fano.

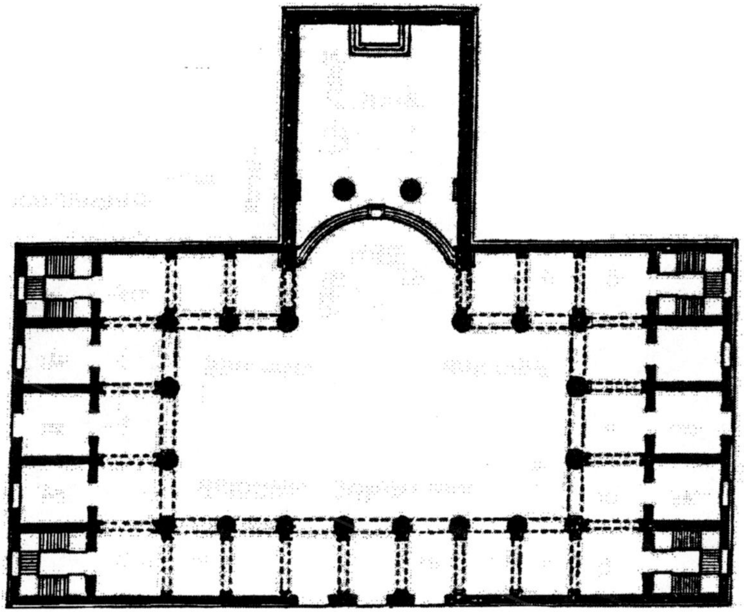

Figure 11. Interior of Sta. Sabina, Rome.

Figure 12. Interior of Santa Maria Maggiore, Rome.

Figure 13. Lepcis Magna, Severan forum with adjacent basilica. Drawing by Macdonald.

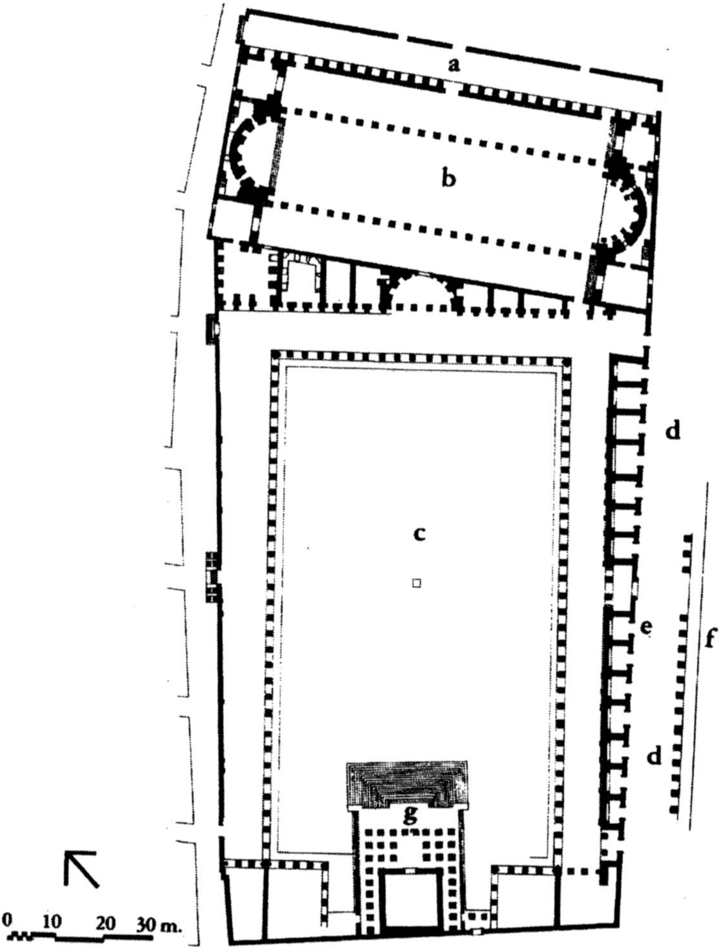

a. side street; b. basilica; c. forum; d. arcaded walkway;
e. shops; f. Severan boulevard;
g. temple to the Severan dynasty

Figure 14. Basilica at Sepphoris, Israel. Drawing by J. F. Strange.

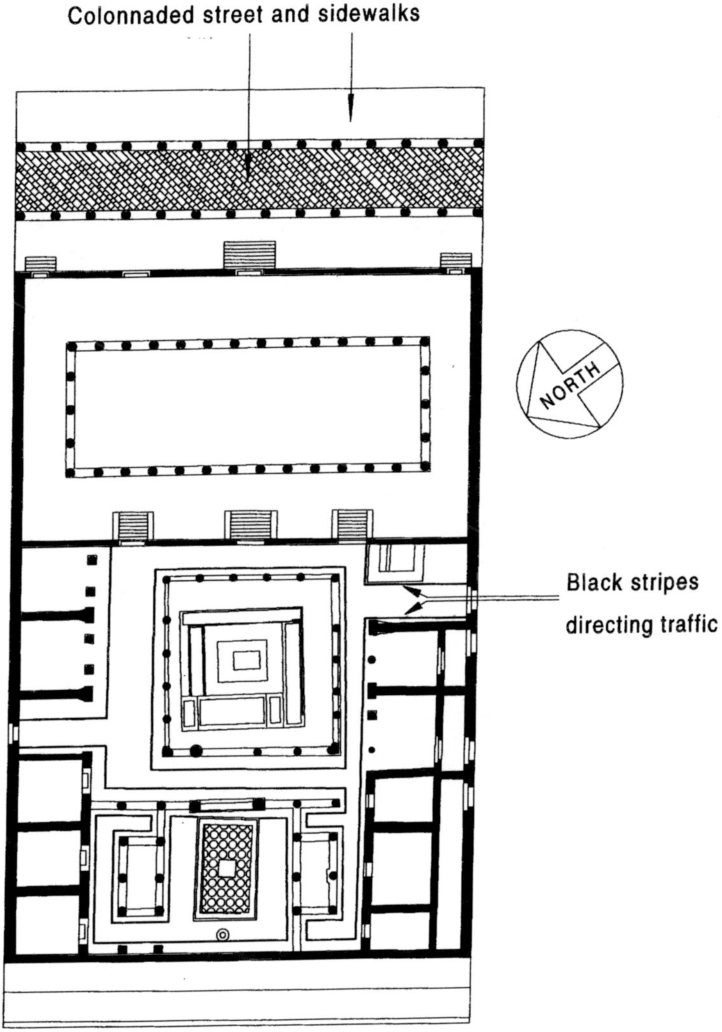

Figure 15. Main east-west thoroughfare, looking west, Timgad.

Figure 16. Arcadiané, Ephesus.

Figure 17. Sarcophagus of Junius Bassus, showing Christ entering Jerusalem (bottom panel) and Christ enthroned over Coelus (top), including Old and New Testament scenes.

Figure 18. Arch of Galerius, detail. Diocletian and Maximian enthroned over the personified sky and earth.

Figure 19. Ivory plaque depicting the resurrected Christ being welcomed into heaven by the hand of God.

Figure 20. Alexandrian bronze coin. The reverse depicts Constantine being welcomed into heaven by the hand of God.

Figure 21. Arch of Constantine, Rome.

Figure 22. Side panel on Arch of Constantine, depicting the Emperor distributing largesse.

Figure 23. Meiron synagogue. After a drawing by Larry Belkin.

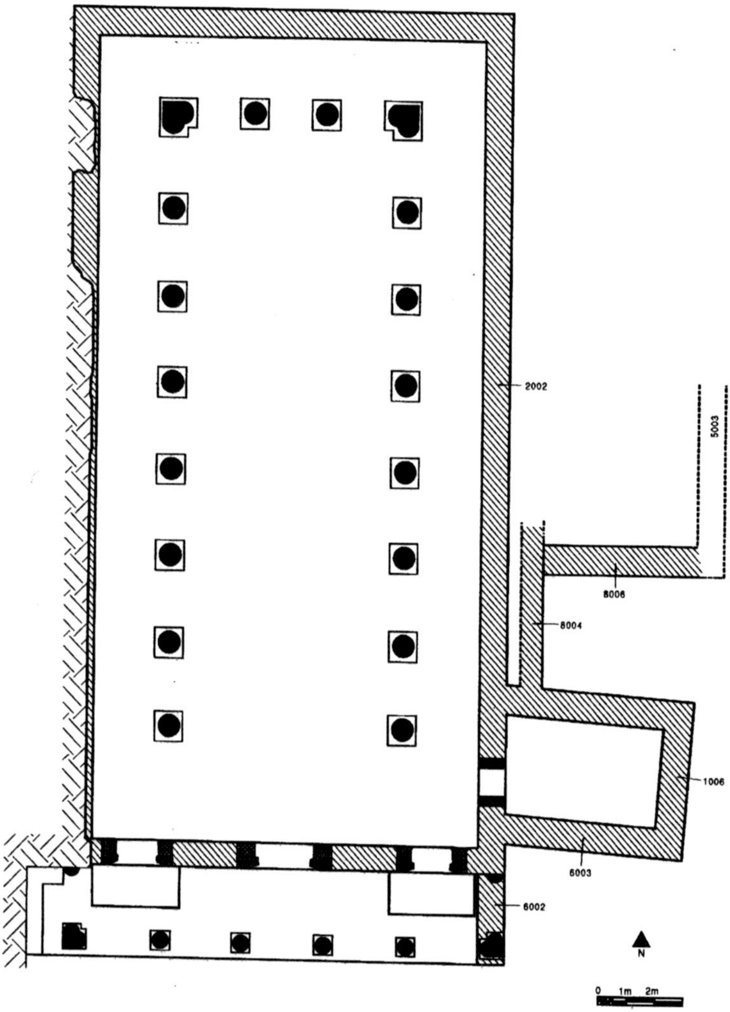

Figure 24. Kh. Shema' synagogue. After a drawing by John Thompson.

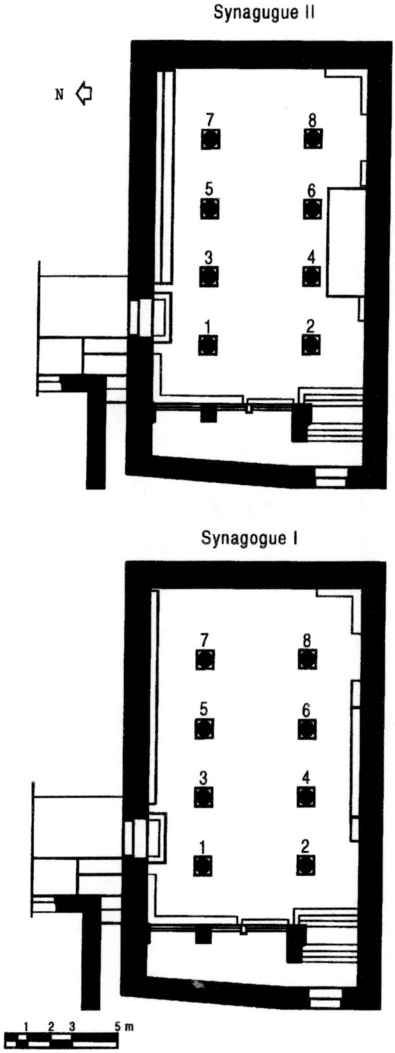

Figure 25. Capernaum synagogue. After a drawing by Corbo.

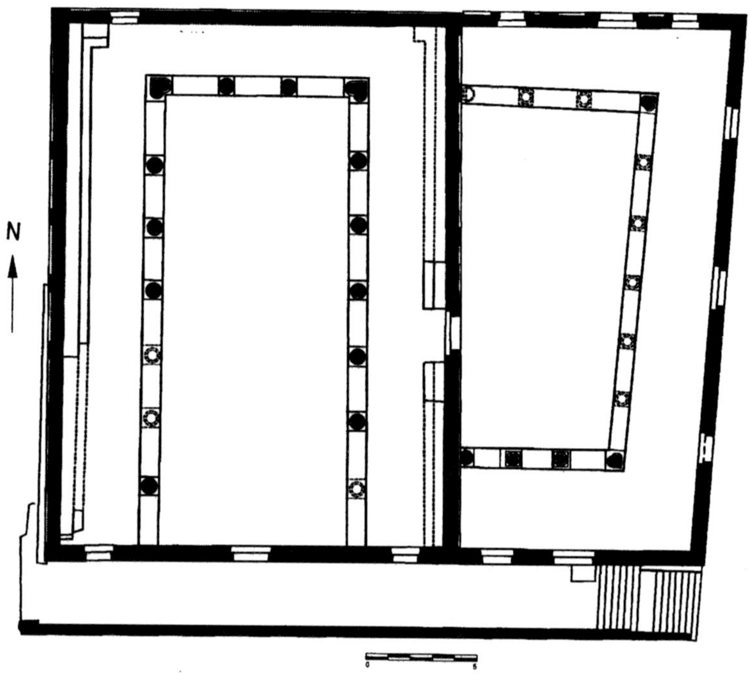

Appendix 2: Ancient Sources

Aland, Barbara, Kurt Aland, Johannes Karavidopoulos, Carlo M. Martini, Bruce Metzger, eds. *The Greek New Testament.* Fourth Revised Edition. Stuttgart: Deutsche Bibelgesellschaft, 1993.

Albeck, H. *Shishah Sidre Mishnah.* Tel Aviv and Jerusalem: Mosad Bialik, 1954-1958.

Clement of Alexandria. *Paedagogus.* Patrologia cursus completus Series Graeca. Vol. 8.

Eusebius. *De vita Constantini imperatoris libri quatuor.* Patrologia cursus completus Series Graeca. Vol. 20.

_____. *Ecclesiastical History.* Translated by C. F. Cruse. Peabody, MA: Hendrickson, 1998.

Fraser, Michael. *Egeria and the Fourth Century Liturgy of Jerusalem.* University of Durham Department of Theology, 1994. On-line hypertext version. Available from http://users.ox.ac.uk/~mikef/durham/egeria.html.

Justin Martyr. *Apologia primus pro Christianis.* Patrologia cursus completus Series Graeca. Vol. 6.

Itinerarium Burdigalense. Corpus scriptorum ecclesiasticorum latinorum. Vol. XXXVIIII. Itinera Hierosolymitana. Saeculi IIII - VIII. ed. P. Geyer. Vienna: F. Tempsky, 1898, 1-33.

S. Siluiae, quae fertur, peregrinatio ad loca sancta. Corpus scriptorum ecclesiasticorum latinorum. Vol. XXXVIIII. Itinera Hierosolymitana. Saeculi IIII - VIII. ed. P. Geyer. Vienna: F. Tempsky, 1898, 35-101.

Vitruvius. *On Architecture.* Ed. and Translated by Frank Granger. 2 Vols. Cambridge, MA: Harvard University Press and London: William Heinemann Ltd., 1983.

______. *The Ten Books on Architecture.* Translated by Morris H. Morgen. New York: Dover Publications, 1960 [Originally published by Harvard University Press in 1914].

Wilkinson, John. *Egeria's Travels.* London: S.P.C.K., 1971.

Appendix 3: Select Bibliography

Bradshaw, Paul F. *The Search for the Origins of Christian Worship: Sources and Methods for the Study of Early Liturgy*. New York: Oxford, 1992.

Carson, R. A. G. *Coins of the Roman Empire*. London and New York: Routledge, 1990.

Cochrane, Charles Norris. *Christianity and Classical Culture: A Study of Thought and Action from Augustus to Augustine*. New York: Oxford University Press, 1957.

Coleman, Simon and John Elsner. "The Pilgrim's Progress: Art, Architecture and Ritual Movement at Sinai." *World Archaeology* 26 No. 1 (June 1994): 73-89.

Corbo, Virgilo C. *Il Santo Sepolcro di Gerusalemme: Aspetti archeologici dalle origini al periodo crociato*. Vol. II. Jerusalem: Franciscan Printing Press, 1981.

Crowfoot, J. W. *Early Churches in Palestine*. College Park, MD: McGrath, 1971.

Davies, J. G. *The Origin and Development of Early Christian Church Architecture*. London: SCM Press Ltd., 1952.

Deissmann, Adolf. *Light from the Ancient East: The New Testament Illustrated by Recently Discovered Texts of the Graeco-Roman World*. Revised. Translated by Lionel R.M. Strachan. Grand Rapids: Baker Books House, 1980. German, 1909.

Di Segni, Leah. "Epigraphic documentation on building in the provinces of *Palestina* and *Arabia*, 4th-7th c." In *The Roman and Byzantine Near East*. Vol. 2. *Some Recent Archaeological Research*. Ed. J. H. Humphrey. Journal of Roman Archaeology, Supplemental Series Number 31. Portsmouth, Rhode Island: Journal of Roman Archaeology, 1999.

Dix, Gregory. *The Shape of the Liturgy.* London: Dacre Press, 1945. Reprint, 1964.

Elbogen, Ismar. *Jewish Liturgy: A Comprehensive History.* Translated by Raymond P. Scheindlin. Philadelphia: The Jewish Publication Society. New York: The Jewish Theological Seminary of America, 1993. German, 1913. Hebrew, 1972.

Encyclopaedia Judaica, s.v. "SIMHAT TORAH".

Goodenough, Erwin R. *Jewish Symbols in the Greco-Roman Period.* Vol. 1. *The Archaeological Evidence from Palestine.* Vol. 3. *Illustrations.* New York: Pantheon Books, 1953.

Gough, Michael. *The Origins of Christian Art.* New York: Praeger Publishers, 1973.

Grabar, André. *Early Christian Art: From the Rise of Christianity to the Death of Theodosius.* Translated by Stuart Gilbert and James Emmons. New York: Odyssey Press, 1968.

Hammond, Peter. *Liturgy and Architecture.* New York: Columbia University Press, 1961.

Hoffman, Lawrence A. *The Canonization of the Synagogue Service.* Notre Dame: University of Notre Dame Press, 1979.

_____. "Jewish Liturgy and Jewish Scholarship." in Judaism in Late Antiquity. Part I, The Literary & Archaeological Sources. Ed. Jacob Neusner. Leiden: E.J. Brill, 1995, 239-66.

Jungmann, Joseph A. *The Mass of the Roman Rite: Its Origin and Development.* 2 Vols. Translated by Francis A. Brunner. Benzinger Brothers, 1951. Replica Edition 1986 by Christian Classics.

Kennedy, Roger G. *American Churches.* New York: Stewart, Tabori, and Chang, 1982.

Kohl, Heinrich and Carl Watzinger. *Antike Synagogen in Galilaea.* Jerusalem: Kedem Publishing, Ltd., 1973. Reprint of 1916 edition, Leipzig.

Krautheimer, Richard. "The Beginning of Early Christian Architecture." *Review of Religion.* III (1939): 127-48. Reprinted in *Studies in Early Christian, Medieval, and Renaissance Art.* New York: New York University Press. London: University of London Press Limited, 1969, 1-20.

______. "The Constantinian Basilica of the Lateran." *Antquity*, XXXIV (1960): 201-6. Reprinted in *Studies in Early Christian, Medieval, and Renaissance Art.* New York: New York University Press; London: University of London Press Limited, 1969. 21-5.

______. *Early Christian and Byzantine Architecture.* Baltimore: Penguine Books, 1965.

Krautheimer, Richard, Wolfgang Frankl, and Spencer Corbett. *Corpus Basilicarum Christianarum Romae: The Early Christian Basilicas of Rome (IV-IX Cent.).* Vols I-V. Rome: Pontificio Instituto di Archeologia Christiana; New York: New York University Press, 1959.

Lang, S. "A few suggestions toward a new solution to the origin of the early christian basilica." *Rivista di archeologia cristiana* 30 (1934): 189-208.

Lietzmann, Hans. *Mass and Lord's Supper: A Study in the History of the Liturgy.* Leiden, Netherlands: Brill, 1979.

Loffreda, S. "The Late Chronology of the Synagogue of Capernaum." *Ancient Synagogues Revealed.* Ed. Lee I. Levine. Jerusalem: Israel Exploration Society, 1981, 52-7.

Macaulay, David. *City: A Story of Roman Planning and Construction.* Boston: Houton Mifflin, 1974.

MacCormack, Sabine G. *Art and Ceremony in Late Antiquity.* Berkeley and Los Angeles, Ca.: University of California Press, 1981.

MacDonald, William L. *The Architecture of the Roman Empire, Volume I: An Introductory Study.* New Haven: Yale University Press, 1965. *Volume II: An Urban Appraisal,* 1986.

_____. *Early Byzantine and Christian Architecture.* New York: George Brasiller, 1982.

Mader, A.E. "Les fouilles allemandes au Ramet El Khalil: la Mambré biblique de la tradition primitive." *Revue Biblique* 39 (1930) 84: 115-7. Figs. 2, 5. Pls. 5, 7.

Mango, Cyril. *Byzantine Architecture.* New York: Harry N. Abrams, 1976.

Matthews, Thomas A. *The Clash of Gods: A Reinterpretation of Early Christian Art.* Revised. Princeton: Princeton University Press, 1993.

Meyers, Eric M., A. Thomas Kraabel, and James F. Strange. *Ancient Synagogue Excavations at Khirbet Shema', Upper Galilee, Israel 1970-1972.* The Annual of the American Schools of Oriental Research. Vol. XLII. Ed. David Noel Freedman. Durham, NC: Duke University Press, 1976.

Meyers, Eric M., James F. Strange, and Carol C. Meyers. *Excavations at Ancient Meiron, Upper Galilee, Israel 1971-72, 1974-75, 1977.* Cambridge, MA: The American Schools of Oriental Research, 1981.

Milburn, Robert. Early Christian Art and Architecture. Berkeley and Los Angeles: University of California Press, 1988.

Neusner, Jacob. *Symbol and Theology in Early Judaism.* Minneapolis: Fortress Press, 1991.

Ovadiah, Asher. *Corpus of the Byzantine Churches in the Holy Land.* Translated by Rose Kirson. Bonn: Peter Hanstein Verlag, 1970.

Ovadiah, Asher, and Carla Gomez de Silva. "Supplementum to the Corpus of the Byzantine Churches in the Holy Land." *Levant* 13 (1981): 200-261. 14 (1982): 122-70. 16 (1984): 129-65.

Richardson, L. Jr. *Pompeii: An Architectural History.* Baltimore: The Johns Hopkins University Press, 1989.

Richmond, E.T. "Basilica of the Nativity: Discovery of the Remains of an Earlier Church." *Quarterly of the Department of Antiquities in Palestine* 5 (1936): 75-81. Pls. 27-48.

_____. "The Church of the Nativity: The Plan of the Constantinian Church." *Quarterly of the Department of Antiquities in Palestine* 6 (1938): 63-72. Pls. 13-17.

Rivoira, G.T. *Roman Architecture and Its Principles of Construction Under the Empire.* New York: Hacker Art Books, 1972.

Schowalter, Daniel N. *The Emperor and the Gods: Images from the Time of Trajan.* Minneapolis: Fortress Press, 1993.

Sear, Frank. *Roman Architecture.* Ithaca: Cornell University Press, 1982.

Setton, Kenneth M. *Christian Attitude Towards the Emperor in the Fourth Century, Especially As Shown in Addresses to the Emperor.* New York: AMS Press, 1967.

Snyder, Graydon F. *Ante Pacem: Archaeological Evidence of Church Life Before Constantine.* Macon: Mercer University Press, 1991.

Strange, James F. "Ancient Texts, Archaeology as Text, and the Problem of the First Century Synagogue." In *Evolution of the Synagogue: Problems and Progress.* Ed. Howard Clark Kee and Lynn H. Cohick. Harrisburg, PA: Trinity Press International, 1999, 27-45.

______. "First Century Galilee from Archaeology and from the Texts." in *Archaeology and the Galilee: Texts and Contexts in the Graeco-Roman and Byzantine Periods.* Ed. Douglas R. Edwards and C. Thomas McCollough. Atlanta: Scholars Press, 1997, 39-48.

______. "The Eastern Basilical Building." In *Sepphoris in Galilee: Crosscurrents in Culture.* Ed. Rebecca Nagy *et al.* North Carolina Museum of Art, 1996, 117-121.

Taylor, Lily Ross. *The Divinity of the Roman Emperor.* Middletown, CT: American Philological Association, 1931.

Tsafrir, Yoram. *Ancient Churches Revealed.* Jerusalem: Israel Exploration Society, 1993.

Urman, Dan, and Paul V. M. Flesher, Eds. *Ancient Synagogues: Historical Analysis and Archaeological Discovery.* Vol. 2. Leiden: E. J. Brill, 1995.

Vincent, H. "L'église de l'éléona." *Revue Biblique* 20 (1911): 219-65. Pls. 1-10.

Ward-Perkins, J. B. "Constantine and the Origins of the Christian Basilica." *Papers of the British School at Rome* 22 (1954): 69-90.

______. *Roman Imperial Architecture.* Middlesex, England: Penguin Books, 1987.

Warren, F. E. *The Liturgy and Ritual of the Ante-Nicene Church.* 2nd Ed. Revised. New York: AMS Press, 1973.

White, James F. and Susan J. White. *Church Architecture: Building and Renovating for Christian Worship.* Nashville: Abingdon Press, 1988.

White, Michael L. *The Social Origins of Christian Architecture.* Vol. I. *Building God's House in the Roman World: Architectural Adaptation among Pagans, Jews and Christians.* Valley Forge, PA: Trinity Press International, 1990. Vol. II, *Texts and Monuments for the Christian Domus Ecclesiae in its Environment,* 1997.

______. *Jerusalem Pilgrims Before the Crusades.* Warminster, England: Aris & Phillips, 1977.

Zahavy, Tzvee. *Studies in Jewish Prayer.* Lanham, MD: University Press of America, 1990.

Appendix 4: Bibliographical Guide to the Study of Early Christian Architecture

Alföldi, A. *The Conversion of Constantine and Pagan Rome.* Oxford: 1948.

Anderson, S. *On Streets.* Cambridge, Mass.: 1978.

Armstrong, Gregory T. "Imperial Church Building and Church-State Relations, A.D. 313-363." *Church History* 37 (1967): 3-17.

_____. "Imperial Church Building in the Holy Land in the Fourth Century." *Biblical Archaeologist* 30 (1967): 90-102.

_____. "Constantine's Churches: Symbol and Structure." *Journal of the Society of Architectural Historians* 33 (1974): 5-16.

Attridge, Harold W. "The Philosophical Critique of Religion under the Early Empire." *Aufstieg und Niedergang der römischen Welt.* 2.16.1 (1979): 45-68.

Avi-Yona, Michael. "Ancient Synagogues." *Ariel, A Quarterly Review of Arts and Letters in Israel* 32 (1973): 29-43. Reprinted in J. Gutmann, ed. *The Synagogue: Studies in Origins, Archaeology and Architecture.* New York: KTAV, 1975.

_____. "Synagogue Architecture." *Encyclopedia Judaica*, 2nd ed. (1971): 15, 593-600.

Bagatti, B. *Gli antichi edifici sacri di Betlemme.* Jerusalem: Studium Biblicum Francescanum, 1951.

_____. "Oggetti inediti de Cafarnao." *Liber Annus de Studium Biblicum Franciscanum* 14 (1964): 261-72.

Baldi, D. *Enchiridion Locorum Sanctorum.* Jerusalem: Studium Biblicum, 1935.

Baldovin, J. *The Urban Character of Christian Worship*. Rome: Orientalia Cristiana Analecta 228, 1986.

Banks, Robert. *Paul's Idea of Community: The Early House Churches in their Historical Setting*. Grand Rapids: Eerdmans, 1980.

Barrett, J. C. "Towards an Archaeology of Ritual." *In Sacred and Profane. Proceedings of a Conference on Archaeology, Ritual and Religion*. Eds. P. Garwood, D. Jennings, R. Skeats, and J. Toms. Oxford: Oxford University Committee for Archaeology, 1991, 1-9.

Barthes, Roland. *Elements of Semiology*. London: Jonathan Cape, 1967.

Bedard, Walter M. *The Symbolism of the Baptismal Font in Early Christian Thought*. Washington: Catholic University of America Press, 1951.

Beilen, Heinz. "Συνγωγὴ τῶν 'Ιουδαίον καὶ θεοσεβῶν, Die Aussage einer bosporanischen Freilassungsinschrift (CIRB 71) zum Problem der 'Gott-fürchtigen'." *Jahrbuch fur Antike und Christentum* 8-9 (1965-66): 171-90.

Bernheimer, R. "An Ancient Oriental Source of Christian Sacred Architecture." *American Journal of Archaeology* 43 (1939): 647-88.

Bieler, Andre. *Architecture in Worship*. Philadelphia: Westminster, 1965.

Blake, M. E. *Roman Construction in Italy from Tiberias through the Flavians*. Washington: CASVA, 1959.

_____. *Roman Construction in Italy from Nerva to the Antonines*. Philadelphia: CASVA, 1973.

Boëthius, A. *Etruscan and Early Roman Architecture*. Harmondsworth, 1978.

_____. "Roman Architecture from its Classicistic to its Late Imperial Phase." *Göteborgs Högskolas Arsskrift* 47,8 (1941).

Bornkamm, Günther. *Early Christian Experience.* Translated by P. L. Hammer. New York: Harper & Row, 1969.

Bovni, Giuseppe. *La proprietà ecclesiastica e la condizione giuridica della chiesa in età preconstantiniana.* Publicazione dei Università di Roma dell'instituto di Diritto Romano 28. Milan: Università di Roma, 1948.

Bradshaw, Paul F. and Lawrence A. Hoffman, eds. *The Making of Jewish and Christian Worship.* Notre Dame: University of Notre Dame Press, 1991.

Broadbent, Geoffrey, Richard Bunt, and Charles Jencks, eds. *Signs, Symbols, and Architecture.* New York: John Wiley & Sons, 1980.

Brown, F. E. *Roman Architecture.* New York: 1961.

Brown, P. "Aspects of the Christianization of the Roman Aristocracy." *Journal of Roman Studies* 51 (1961): 1-11.

Bultmann, Rudolf. *Primitive Christianity in its Contemporary Setting.* Translated by R. H. Fuller. Cleveland, OH: Meridian Books, 1956.

Capelle, B. "L'introduction du catéchumenat à Rome. Translated by E. O. Lorimer. New Haven: Yale University Press, 1959.

Case, Shirley Jackson. *The Social Origins of Christianity.* Chicago: University of Chicago Press, 1923.

Cecchelli, Carlo. "Il problema della basilica cristiana preconstantiniana." *Palladio* 7 (1943): 1-18.

Chevallier, R. *Roman Roads.* London: 1976.

Cobb, Peter J. "The Architectural Setting of the Liturgy." In *The Study of Liturgy.* rev. ed. ed. Cheslyn Jones *et al.* New York: Oxford University Press, 1992, 528-42.

Coche de la Ferté, E. "Basilica." *Enciclopedia dell'arte antica* 2 (1959): 2-15.

Coleman, C. B. *The Treatize of Lorenzo Valla on the Donation of Constantine.* New Haven: 1922.

Colemen, S. M. and J. Elsner. "Contesting Pilgrimage." *Cambridge Anthropology* 15, no. 3 (1991): 63-73.

Cooper, K. "Institutions of Womanly Influence: An Aspect of the Christianization of the Roman Aristocracy." *Journal of Roman Studies* 82 (1992): 150-64.

Corbo, Virgilio. *The House of St. Peter at Capharnaum, a preliminary report of the first two campaigns of Excavations, 1968.* Translated by S. Saller. Studium Biblicum Franciscanum, Collectio minor 5. Jerusalem: Studium Biblicum Franciscanum, 1969.

Coüasnon, C., o.p. *The Church of the Holy Sepulchre in Jerusalem. The Schweich Lectures 1972.* London: 1974.

Coulton, J. J. *The Architectural Development of the Greek Stoa.* Chapter 9. Oxford: Oxford University Press, 1976.

Countryman, L. William. "The Rich Christian in the Church of the Early Empire: Contradictions and Accommodations." Texts and Studies in Religion. New York: Edwin Mellen, 1980.

Crema. L. *L'architettura romana.* BollCentro 15. Turin: 1959.

_____. *Significato della architettura romana.* Rome: 1959.

Davies, J. G. *The Architectural Setting of Baptism.* London: Barrie & Rockliff, 1962.

_____. "Architectural Setting." In *The New Westminster Dictionary of Liturgy and Worship.* ed. J. G. Davies. Philadelphia: Westminster, 1986, 26-36.

_____. "Architecture and Theology." *Expository Times* 73 (1962): 231-33.

_____. *The Early Christian Church.* New York: Anchor Books, 1967.

_____. *The Origin and Development of Early Christian Architecture.* London: SCM Press, 1952.

_____. *The Secular Use of Church Buildings.* New York: Seabury, 1968.

_____. *Temples, Churches, and Mosques: A Guide to the Appreciation of Religious Architecture.* New York: Pilgrim, 1982.

Dehio, G. *Die Genesis der christilichen Basilica.* Sitzungsbericht der k. bayerishen Akademie der Wissenschaften, phil.-historiche Klasse 12. Munich: Kaiser, 1882.

Dehio, G. and G. von Bezold. *Die kirchliche Kunst des Abendlandes, I.* Stuttgart: 1884.

Deichmann, F. W. "Basilica." In Theodore Dlauser, ed. *Reallexikon für Antike und Christentum*, 1. 1225-59. Leipzig and Stuttgart: J. C. Hinrichs, 1941ff.

_____. "Von Tempel zur Kirche." *Mullus: Festschrift Theodor Klauser.* JAC Erganzungsband 1. Münster: Aschendorff, 1964.

Dodds, J. D. *Architecture and Ideology in Early Medieval Spain.* Pennsylvania: Pennsylvania State University Press, 1990.

Donnay-Rocmans, C. "'Basilique' dans la litterature chrétienne d'Afrique au Ives." *Annuaire de l'Institut de Philologie et d'histoire orientales et slaves* 15 (1960): 153-62.

Downey, Glanville. "The words STOA and BASILIKE in Classical Literature. *American Journal of Archeology* (1937): 41-205.

Dyggve, E. *Basilica Discoperta: Zeitschrift für Kirchengeshichte* 59 (1940).

Eade, J. and S. Sallnow, eds. *Contesting the Sacred: The Anthropology of Christian Pilgrimage.* London: Routledge, 1991.

Eck, Werner. "Das Eindringen der Christentums in den Senatorenstand bis zu Konstantin d. Gr." *Chiron* 1 (1971): 381-406.

Eco, Umberto., "Functions and Sign: The Semioctics of Architecture." In *Signs, Symbols and Architecture.* Ed. Geoffry Broadbent, Richard Bunt, and Charles Jencks. New York: John Wiley & Sons, 1980.

———. *A Theory of Semiotics.* Bloomington: Indiana University Press, 1979.

Feldman, L. H. "The Significance of Early Christian House Churches." *Journal of Biblical Literature* 58 (1939): 105-12.

Finkelstein, Louis. "The Origin of the Synagogue." *Proceedings of the American Academy for Jewish Research* 1 (1928-30): 49-59. Reprinted in J. Gutman, ed. *The Synagogue: Studies in Origins, Archaeology and Architecture.* New York: KTAV, 1975.

Finney, Paul Corby. "TOPOS HIEROS und christlicher Sakralbau in vorkonstantinischer Überlieferung." *BOREAS: Münstersche Beiträge zur Archäologie* 7 (1984): 193-223.

———. "Early Christian Architecture: The Beginnings (A Review Article)." *Harvard Theological Review* 81 (1988): 319-39.

Forester, G. "Notes on Recent Excavations at Capernaum." *Israel Exploration Journal* 21 (1971): 207-11.

Fortlati, F. "L'architettura della basilica." *La Basilica di Aquileia.* Comitato per ceremonie celebrative del IX. Centrenario della Basilica. Bologna: il Mulino, 1933.

Fototeca Unione. *Ancient Roman Architecture.* 2 vols. Chicago: 1979, 1982; ca. 24,000 microfiches of Roman sites and buildings.

Gager, John G. "Christianity and Social Class in the Early Roman Empire." In S. Benko and J. J. O'Rourke, eds. *The Catacombs and the Colosseum: The Roman Empire as the Setting of Primitive Christianity.* Valley Forge, PA: Judson, 1971.

_____. *Kingdom and Community: The Social World of Early Christianity.* Englewood Cliffs, NJ: Prentice-Hall, 1975.

Geanakoplos, Deno J. "Church Building and 'Caesaropapism,' A.D. 312-565." *Greek, Roman and Byzantine Studies* 7 (1966): 167-86.

Glück, H. "Herkunft des Querschiffes in der Römischen Basilica und der Trichonkos." In *Fetschrift für Paul Clemen.* Bonn: 1926.

Grabar, A. "Christian Architecture, East and West." *Archaeology* 2 (1949): 95-104.

_____. *Martyrium. Recherches sur le culte des reliques et l'art chrétien antique, I.* Paris: 1946.

Grant, Robert M. *Augustus to Constantine: The Thrust of the Christian Movement into the Roman World.* New York: Macmillan, 1970.

_____. *Early Christianity and Society.* New York: Harper & Row, 1977.

_____. "Eusebius H.E. VIII: Another Suggestion." *Vigilae Christianae* 22 (1968): 16-18.

_____. "The Social Setting of Second Century Christianity." In E. P. Sanders, ed. *Jewish and Christian Self-Definition.* Vol. 1: *The Shaping of Christianity in the Second and Third Centuries.* Philadelphia: Fortress, 1980.

_____. "Temples, Churches and Endowments." In *Early Christianity and Society.* New York: Harper & Row, 1977.

Günter, R. *Wand, Fenster und Licht in der spätantikfrühchristlichen Architecktur.* Herford: 1965.

Gutman, Joseph, ed. *Ancient Synagogues: The State of Research.* Brown Judaic Studies 23. Chico, CA: Scholars Press, 1981.

_____, ed. *The Synagogue: Studies in Origins, Archaeology and Architecture.* New York: KTAV, 1975.

Han, Ferdinand. *The Worship of the Early Church.* Translated by D. E. Green. Philadelphia: Fortress, 1973.

Harvey, W. "Recent Discoveries at the Church of the Nativity, Bethlehem." *Archaeologia* 87 (1937): 7-18.

———. *Structural Survey of the Church of the Nativity, Bethlehem.* Oxford: Oxford University Press, 1935.

Hengel, Martin. *Property and Riches in the Early Church.* Translated by J. Bowden. Philadelphia: Fortress, 1974.

———. "Proseuche und Synagoge: Judische Gemeinde, Gotteshaus, und Gottesdienst in der Diaspora und in Palastina." In J. Gutman, ed. *The Synagogue: Studies in Origins, Archaeology, and Architecture.* New York: KTAV, 1975.

Hinson, E. Glenn. *The Evangelization of the Roman Empire: Identity and Adaptability.* Macon, GA: Mercer University Press, 1981.

Hodder, I. *Reading the Past: Current Approaches to Interpretation in Archaeology.* Cambridge: Cambridge University Press, 1986.

Holum, K. "Hadrian and St. Helena: Imperial Travel and the Origins of Christian Holy Land Pilgrimage." In *The Blessings of Pilgrimage.* Ed. R. Ousterhout. Illinois Byzantine Studies 1. Urbana and Chicago: University of Illinois Press, 1990, 66-81.

Humphrey, C. "No Place Like Home in Anthropology. The Neglect of Architecture." *Anthropology Today* 4, no. 1 (1988): 16-18.

Hunt, E. D. *Holy Land Pilgrimage in the Later Roman Empire A.D. 312-460.* Oxford: Oxford University Press, 1982.

Huttmann, Maude A. *The Establishment of Christianity and the Proscription of Paganism.* New York: Columbia University Press, 1914.

Jencks, Charles and George Baird, eds. *Meaning in Architecture.* London: Barrie & Jenkins, 1969. Reprint 1970.

Jones, Arnold Hugh Martin. *The Cities of the Eastern Roman Provinces.* 2nd ed. Oxford: Clarendon, 1971.

_____. *Constantine and the Conversion of Europe.* New York: Macmillan, 1948. Reprint, Toronto: Toronto University Press, 1978.

_____. *The Later Roman Empire 284-602: A Social, Economic, and Administrative Survey.* 2 vols. Norman, OK: University of Oklahoma Press, 1964.

Jones, Cheslyn *et al.* eds. *The Study of Liturgy.* rev. ed. New York: Oxford University Press, 1992.

Jungmann, Josef A. *The Early Liturgy to the Time of Gregory the Great.* Notre Dame, Ind: Notre Dame University Press, 1959.

Kautsky, Karl. *Foundatios of Christianity, A Study in Christian Origins.* Translated from the 13th German ed. New York: Monthly Review, 1972.

Kavanagh, Aidan. "The Church Building as a Setting for Liturgical Action." In *The Complete Library of Christian Worship.* vol. 4. *Music and the Arts in Christian Worship.* ed. Robert Webber. Nashville: Star Song, 1994, 557-59.

Keck, Leander E. "On the Ethos of the Early Christians." *Journal of the American Academy of Religion* 42 (1974): 435-52.

Kirsch, J. P. "Das Querschiff in den stadtrömischen christlichen Basiliken des Altertums." *Pisciculi* (Munster i. W. 1939).

_____"Die Entwicklung des Bautypus der altchristlichen römischen Basiliken." *Römische Quartalschrift* 43 (1935).

_____. *Die römische Titelkirchen im Altertum.* Paderborn: Schönigh, 1918.

Kitschelt, L. *Die altschristliche Basilika als eine Darstellung des Himmlishcen Jerusalems.* Munich: 1938.

Klauck, Hans-Josef. *Hausgemeinde und Hauskirche im frühen Christentum.* Stuttgart: Katholisches Bibelwerk, 1981.

Klauser, Th. "Die konstantinischen Altäre der Lateransbasilia." *Römische Quartalschrift* 43 (1935).

Krampen, Martin. "Survey on Current Work in Semiology of Architecture." In *A Semiotic Landscape: Proceedings of the First Congress of the International Association for Semiotic Studies.* ed. Seymour Chatman, Umberto Eco, and Jean-Marie Klinkenberg. International Association for Semiotic Studies. New York: Mouton, Milan, June, 1974, 1969. Reprint, 1970.

Lang, S. "A Few Suggestions Toward a New Solution of the Origin of the Early Christian Basilica." *Rivista di archeologia cristiana* 30 (1954): 189-208.

von Lange, K. *Haus und Halle.* Leipzig: J. C. Hinrichs, 1885.

Lassus, Jean. "Les edifices du culte autour de la basilique." *Atti VI CIAC (1962).* Vatican City: Pontifici Istituto de archeologia cristiana, 1965.

Lawlor, Hugh Jackson. *Eusebiana: Essays on the Ecclesiastical History of Eusebius Pamphilii, ca. 264-349, Bishop of Caesarea.* Oxford: Clarendon, 1912.

Leclercq, Henri. "Basilique." In F. Cabrol and H. Leclercq, eds. *Dictionaire du archeologie chrétienne et la liturgie*, 2. cols., col. 525-602. Paris: Letouzey et Ané, 1907-51.

Lemaire, R. *L'Origine de la basilique Latine.* Brussels: Lamertin, 1911.

Liesenberg, K. *Der Einfluss der Liturgie auf die frühchristliche Basilika.* Neustadt: a. d. Haardt, 1928.

Loerke, W. "'Real Presence' in Early Christian Art." In *Monasticism and the Arts.* Ed. T. G. Verdun. Syracuse, NY: Syracuse University Press, 1984.

Lowrie, Walter. *Art in the Early Church.* Rev. ed. New York: Pantheon, 1947.

Lukken, Gerard and Mark Searle. *Semiotics and Church Architecture: Applying the Semiotics of A. J. Greimas and the Paris School to the Analysis of Church Buildings.* The Netherlands: Kok Pharos Publishing House, 1993.

MacDonald, W. L. "Roman Architects." In S. Kostof, ed. *The Architect. Chapters in the History of the Profession.* New York: 1977.

Maguire, H. *Earth and Ocean: The Terrestrial World in Early Byzantine Art.* University Park and London: Pennsylvania State University Press, 1987.

MacMullen, Ramsay. *Christianizing the Roman Empire.* New Haven: Yale University Press, 1984.

Malherbe, Abraham J. *Social Aspects of Early Christianity.* 2nd ed. Philadelphia: Fortress, 1983.

Markus, R. A. "The Problem of Self-Definition: From Sect to Church." In E. P. Sanders, ed. *Jewish and Christian Self-Definition*, vol. 1: *The Shaping of Christianity in the Second and Third Centuries*, 1-15. Philadelphia: Fortress, 1980.

Marrou, Henri Irenee. "La basilique chrétienne d'Hippone d'après le résultat des dernièrs fouilles." *Revue des Études Augustiniennes* 6 (1960) 109-54.

Matthews, Thomas, F. *The Early Churches of Constantinople: Architecture and Liturgy.* University Park, Pa.: Pennsylvania State University Press, 1971.

Nassivera, J. C. "Ancient Temples to Pagan Goddesses and Early Churches to the Virgin in the City of Rome." *Échos du monde classique* 20 (1976): 41-54.

Nock, Arthur Darby. *Conversion: The Old and the New in Religion from Alexander the Great to Augustine of Hippo.* London: Oxford University Press, 1933.

_____. *Early Gentile Christianity in its Hellenistic Background.* New York: Harper, 1964.

Ousterhout, R., ed. *The Blessings of Pilgrimage.* Illinois Byzantine Studies 1. Urbana and Chicago: University of Illinois Press, 1990.

Penella, R. J. "Alexander Serverus 43.6-7: Two Emperors and Christ." *Vigiliae Christianae* 31 (1977): 229-30.

Peterson, J. M. "House Churches in Rome." *Vigiliae Christianae* 23 (1969): 264-72.

Pevsner, N. *A History of Building Types.* London: Thames & Hudson, 1986.

Plommer, H. *Vitruvius and Later Roman Building Manuals.* Cambridge: 1973.

Pollitt, J. J. *The Art of Rome, c. 753 B.C.-337 A.D.* Englewood Cliffs, N.J.: 1966.

Pringle, D. "The Planning of Some Pilgrimage Churches in Crusader Palestine." *World Archaeology* 18, no. 3 (1987): 341-62.

Rakob, F. "Römischen Architektur." In T. Kraus, ed. *Das römische Weltreich.* Propyläen Kunstgeschichte 2. Berlin: 1967.

Rodwell, W., ed. *Temples, Churches, and Religion.* British Archeological Reports 77. London: Oxford University Press, 1980.

Rodorf, Willy. "Was wissen wir über die christlichen Gottesdienstraum der vorkonstantinischen Zeit?" *Zeitschrift für die neutestamentliche Wissenschaft* 55 (1964): 110-28.

Rutgers, Leonard V. *The Jews in Late Ancient Rome: Evidence of Cultural Interaction in the Roman Diaspora.* Leiden: Brill, 1995.

Sanders, E. P., ed. *Jewish and Christian Self-Definition*, vol. 1: *The Shaping of Christianity in the Second and Third Centuries.* Philadelphia: Fortress, 1980.

Sanders, E. P., A. Baumgarten, and A. Mendelson, eds. *Jewish and Christian Self-Definition*, vol. 2: *Aspects of Judaism in the Graeco-Roman Period.* Philadelphia: Fortress, 1981.

Sanders, E. P., and B. F. Meyers, eds. *Jewish and Christian Self-Definition.* Vol. 3. *Self-Definition in the Graeco-Roman World.* Philadelphia: Fortress, 1982.

Schultze, M. V. *Archäologie der altchristlichen Kunst.* Munich: Kaiser, 1895.

Selhorst, H. *Die Plätzanordnung im Glaubigenraum der altchristlichen Kirche.* Münster: Aschendorff, 1931.

Shanks, Hershel. *Judaism in Stone: The Archeology of Ancient Synagogues.* New York: Harper & Row, 1979.

Sivan, H. "Pilgrimage, Monasticism and the Emergence of Christian Palestine in the Fourth Century." In R. Ousterhout, ed. *The Blessings of Pilgrimage.* Urbana and Chicago: University of Illinois Press, 1990, 54-65.

Stambaugh, John E. "The Functions of Roman Temples." *Aufstieg und Niedergang der römischen Welt* 2.16.1 (1978): 554-607.

_____. *The Ancient Roman City.* Baltimore: Johns Hopkins University Press, 1988.

Stopford, J. "Some Approaches to the Archaeology of Christian Pilgrimage." *World Archaeology* 26, no. 1 (June, 1994): 57-72.

Swift, Emerson H. *Roman Sources of Christian Art.* New York: Columbia University Press, 1951.

Testini, P. *Archeologia Cristiana: Nozioni generali dalle origini alla fine del sec. VI.* Rome: Desclée e soc., 1972.

Tsafrir, Y. "The Byzantine Setting and its Influence on Ancient Synagogues." In L. I. Levine ed. *The Synagogue in Late Antiquity.* Philadelphia: 1987, 147-57.

_____. *Eretz Israel from the Destruction of the Second Temple to the Muslim Conquest.* II. *Archaeology and Art.* Jerusalem: 1984.

Turner, Harold W. *From Temple to Meeting House: The Phenomenology and Theology of Places of Worship.* Religion and Society 16. The Hague: Mouton, 1979.

Turner, V. *Dramas, Fields and Metaphors: Symbolic Action in Human Society.* Cornell: Cornell University Press, 1974.

Turner, V. W. and Turner, E. *Image and Pilgrimage in Christian Culture: Anthropological Perspectives.* Oxford: Blackwell, 1978.

Vincent, H. "Bethléem sanctuaire de la nativité, d'après les fouilles récentes." *Revue Biblique* 45 (1936): 551-74; 46 (1937): 93-121.

Voelkl, Ludwig. "Die konstantinischen Kirchenbauten nach Eusebius." *Rivista di archeologia cristiana* 29 (1953): 60-94.

_____. "Die konstantinischen Kirchenbauten nach den literarischen Quellen des Okzidents." *Rivista di archeologia cristiana* 30 (1954): 99-136.

Vogt, Joseph. "Pagans and Christians in the Family of Constantine the Great." In A. Momigliano, ed. *The Conflict of Paganism with Christianity in the Fourth Century.* Oxford: Clarendon, 1963.

Ward-Perkins, J. B. "The Italian Element in Late Roman and Early Mediaeval Architecture." *Proceedings of the British Academy* 33 (London, 1949).

Wharton, A. J. "The Baptistry of the Holy Sepulcher in Jerusalem and the Politics of Sacred Landscape. *Dumbarton Oaks Papers* 46 (1992), 313-25.

Wilken, Robert L. *The Christians as the Romans Saw Them.* New Haven: Yale University Press, 1985.

Wilkinson, J. "Architectural Procedures in Byzantine Palestine." *Levant* 13(1981): 156-72.

Wischnitzer, Rachel. *The Architecture of the European Synagogue.* Philadelphia: Jewish Publication Society, 1974.

Zeitlin, S. "The Origins of the Synagogue." In J. Gutmann, ed. *The Synagogue: Studies in Origins, Archaeology and Architecture.* New York: KTAV, 1975.

Zestermann, A. C. *Die antike und christlichen Basiliken.* Leipzig: J. C. Heinrichs, 1847.

Index